THE WAY
FOR A
CHRISTIAN
TO MATURE
IN LIFE

WITNESS LEE

Living Stream Ministry
Anaheim, California

First Edition, September 2002.

ISBN 0-7363-1965-4

Published by

Living Stream Ministry
2431 W. La Palma Ave., Anaheim, CA 92801 U.S.A.
P. O. Box 2121, Anaheim, CA 92814 U.S.A.

Printed in the United States of America

02   03   04   05   06   07   08 / 9   8   7   6   5   4   3   2   1

CONTENTS

PREFACE

This book is a collection of messages given by Brother Witness Lee in Taipei in 1955. It contains fourteen messages that show us that the way for a Christian to mature in life is by allowing God to build Himself into him, by paying the price before God, by being watchful and ready, by turning to the spirit, and by giving the ground to the Lord.

CHAPTER ONE

THE HOLY CITY, NEW JERUSALEM—
THE FINAL DESTINATION OF THE BELIEVERS

There are records in both the Old Testament and the New Testament that show us where a believer's spirit and soul go after he dies. Most people have the concept that a believer goes to a heavenly mansion immediately after he dies. This, however, is not the thought of the Bible.

In fact, the term *heavenly mansion* that people commonly use is not a biblical term. The Bible speaks of the third heaven (2 Cor. 12:2) and the holy city, New Jerusalem (Rev. 21:2), but neither place is a heavenly mansion as most people think. The word that is translated as *heavenly mansion* in Hebrews 9:24 and 1 Peter 3:22 of the Chinese Union Version should be translated as *heaven*. This word has no connotation of a heavenly mansion. The third heaven is where God dwells today, and the holy city, New Jerusalem, is the ultimate mutual habitation of God and the redeemed ones throughout the generations. Simply speaking, all those who have been saved will eventually enter the holy city of God. When the believers die, their spirits and souls do not enter a heavenly mansion but rather go first to Paradise in Hades (Luke 16:23; 23:43). When the Lord Jesus comes again, they will be resurrected, and their spirits, souls, and bodies will ultimately be united to have a part in the New Jerusalem. We all must be able to clearly discern these points.

THE THREE STAGES FROM
A PERSON'S SALVATION TO ETERNITY

A believer goes through three stages from the time that he is saved until the time that he enters the holy city. His living on the earth is one stage. When he dies and is buried in the ground, his spirit and soul depart from the world. This is another stage. When the Lord Jesus comes again, a believer's spirit and soul will come out of Paradise and his body will come out from the grave; his whole being will thus be resurrected. This is the third stage. Therefore, a believer goes through three different stages from the time he is saved until eternity. In the first stage his body, soul, and spirit live in the world. This is the stage in which he lives on the earth. In the second stage his spirit and soul are separated from his body, that is, his body remains in the grave while his spirit and soul depart to a pleasant place. This is the stage in which he sleeps, or in other words, is physically dead. In the third stage when the Lord Jesus comes again, the believer will be resurrected. His spirit and soul will be reunited with his body, and he will also be transfigured. This is the stage of resurrection, the stage of eternity, in which he will be with the Lord forever.

Today Christianity generally says that when a believer dies, his spirit and soul go to a heavenly mansion but his body remains in the grave without being resurrected. Then when the day of resurrection comes, his body will also go to the heavenly mansion. We have to find out whether this kind of saying is accurate and based on the Scriptures. According to the Bible, when the Lord Jesus comes again, the believer's body, spirit, and soul will be united in resurrection, and he will be transfigured (1 Cor. 15:52). While the believer is alive, he neither goes up to heaven nor goes down to Hades but rather lives on the earth. When he dies, his body is buried in a grave, but where do his spirit and soul go? We have to find the answer.

WHEN A BELIEVER DIES, HIS SPIRIT AND SOUL GOING NOT TO A HEAVENLY MANSION BUT TO PARADISE IN HADES

All those who have been saved will ultimately have a part in the New Jerusalem; this is the scriptural truth. Being in the New Jerusalem does not depend on one's own effort. Rather, it depends altogether on the Lord's salvation. Christianity, however, says that when a believer dies, his spirit and soul immediately go to a heavenly mansion. This kind of speaking is erroneous according to Luke 16. When a believer dies, his spirit and soul actually descend to Paradise in Hades (v. 23). After a believer dies, and before he is resurrected, his spirit and soul go down to a pleasant place in Hades instead of going to a heavenly mansion. This conclusion contradicts the traditional theology of today's Christianity. We must therefore study this matter in the Bible from Genesis in the Old Testament to Revelation in the New Testament.

THE SPIRITS AND SOULS OF THE OLD TESTAMENT SAINTS HAVING GONE TO HADES WHEN THEY DIED

Genesis 42:38 says, "Then you will bring down my gray hairs in sorrow to Sheol." These were Jacob's words. No Christian can deny that Jacob was a saved person. Romans 9:13 says that Jacob was loved by God. Since Jacob was loved and chosen by God, whatever Jacob told us was inspired by the Holy Spirit. Jacob said that he would go in sorrow to Sheol, which is equal to Hades in the New Testament. Perhaps some would say, "This is because Jacob was a bad person who could not be compared with his father, Isaac, and much less with his grandfather, Abraham. It is right for a person like him to go down to Hades. Abraham, however, probably did not go down to Hades." Nevertheless, Genesis 49:33 says that Jacob "expired, and he was gathered to his people." Jacob was gathered to his people. In other words, he went to the place where Abraham and Isaac were. This shows us that Abraham, Isaac, and Jacob are in Hades and not in a heavenly mansion.

Although we all would like to go to a heavenly mansion and may not like to go to Hades, the Bible clearly tells us that when the Old Testament saints died, their spirits and souls went down to Hades. This includes Abraham, Isaac, and Jacob. Psalm 16:10 says, "For You will not abandon my soul to Sheol." This is not only a prophecy concerning the Lord Jesus but also a reference to David, a saint in the Old Testament. According to this word, the Old Testament saints admitted that their souls would go down to Hades at the time of their death. The statement *You will not abandon my soul to Sheol* tells us two things. First, it tells us that their souls would go to Hades and second, that their souls would not be abandoned to Hades. This means that although their souls would go to Hades, they would be resurrected one day and would therefore not be abandoned to Hades. Thus, this was the faith of the Old Testament saints concerning this matter. They believed that when a person died, his spirit and soul went down to Hades, but that at a certain time it would be resurrected and come out of Hades and, therefore, would not be abandoned to Hades. This proves that the Old Testament saints acknowledged that the spirit and soul of a person go to Hades at his death.

THE TWO PARTS OF HADES

In the New Testament the Lord Jesus tells us a story in Luke 16. In this story there are two men—a rich man and a beggar named Lazarus. When the time came, the rich man died, was buried, and was in torment in Hades (vv. 19-23). Perhaps some may say that it was proper for this rich man to go to Hades since he was an unsaved person. Yet Lazarus who was saved also went to Hades at his death, because it says that in Hades the rich man "lifted up his eyes...and saw Abraham from afar and Lazarus in his bosom. And he called out and said, Father Abraham, have mercy on me and send Lazarus to dip the tip of his finger in water and cool my tongue, because I am in anguish in this flame. But Abraham said, Child, remember that in your lifetime you fully received your good things, and Lazarus likewise bad things; but now he is comforted here, and you are in anguish" (vv. 23-25). Here we are told that the rich man went to Hades and that Lazarus was also in Hades. We cannot say that Lazarus was in a heavenly mansion at that time because the rich man saw Lazarus in Abraham's bosom. Moreover, while he was in the flames in Hades, the rich man could talk to Abraham, who was in a place of comfort. This shows us that they were somewhat near each other. Although they were separated by a great chasm, they could talk to each other and hear each other.

In the Old Testament Genesis says that Jacob went to Sheol after his death and went to be with his fathers, one of whom was Abraham. This indicates that Abraham was in Hades, which is also called Sheol. Then in the New Testament when we come to Luke 16, and it says that Abraham was in Hades, except that Abraham was in a place of comfort, as was Lazarus who was also saved. This indicates that there are different sections in Hades. According to Luke, there is a section of Hades that is full of flames and where the spirits and souls of the unsaved ones go to be tormented after they die. There is also another section where Abraham is and where the spirits and souls of the saved ones go to be comforted after they die. Although there is a difference, they are both in Hades. This is what Genesis in the Old Testament and Luke in the New Testament show us.

PARADISE NOT BEING A HEAVENLY MANSION

In Luke 23 the repentant robber who was being crucified said to the Lord Jesus, "Jesus, remember me when You come into Your kingdom." And Jesus said to him, "Truly I say to you, Today you shall be with Me in Paradise" (vv. 42-43). This word clearly shows us that on the same day that the Lord Jesus died, the robber went with Him to Paradise.

Is Paradise a heavenly mansion? Some may say that Paradise is not Hades but a heavenly mansion. They may think that on the day the Lord Jesus died, the robber went with Him to a heavenly mansion. However, Matthew 12:40 says, "For just as Jonah was in the belly of the great fish three days and three nights, so will the Son of Man be in the heart of the earth three days and three nights." The Lord died and was in the heart of the earth for three days and three nights. Immediately after the Lord yielded up His spirit on the cross, His spirit and soul departed from His body, not to go to a heavenly mansion but to Hades, and stayed in the heart of the earth for three days and three nights.

Acts 2:31 says, "He, seeing this beforehand, spoke concerning the resurrection of the Christ, that neither was He abandoned to Hades." After reading Matthew 12:40 some may think that the Lord Jesus being in the heart of the earth refers to His body being buried in the earth and not to His spirit and soul being in Hades. However, concerning the resurrection of Christ

Acts says that His spirit and soul were not abandoned to Hades, showing us that after the Lord died, His spirit and soul went to Hades. The Lord Jesus clearly told the robber, "Today you shall be with Me in Paradise." Paradise is a section of Hades. From Genesis to Acts we are told that the spirits and souls of all the saved ones throughout the generations go to a place of rest in Hades after death. This place is the Paradise in Hades. There is not a shadow of doubt concerning this matter.

TO DEPART AND BE WITH CHRIST
NOT BEING TO GO TO HEAVEN

In Philippians 1:23 Paul says, "But I am constrained between the two, having the desire to depart and be with Christ, for this is far better." Some people may ask, "When Paul talked about departing and being with Christ, was he not talking about going to heaven? Surely Christ is in heaven, so Paul's departing to be with Christ should have been his going to heaven." This sounds fairly reasonable. Furthermore, they may say, "Paul also said that this was far better. Thus, he surely must have been referring to going to heaven because there is nothing better than this." We must tell them, however, that Paul was not referring to going to heaven. Matthew 28:20 tells us that the Lord will be with us until the consummation of the age. Similarly, Paul did not think that to be with Christ was something extraordinary. The Lord is already with us on the earth today. Does this mean that today we are in heaven? To say that to have the presence of Christ is to be in "heaven" is merely a figurative expression. You do not have to wait until you die to go to "heaven." The Lord's presence is available at all times and in all places.

TO BE ABROAD FROM THE BODY AND AT HOME
WITH THE LORD NOT BEING TO GO TO HEAVEN

Second Corinthians 5:8 says, "We are of good courage then and are well pleased rather to be abroad from the body and at home with the Lord." This indicates that to be abroad from the body is to be at home with the Lord. Verse 6 says, "Knowing that while we are at home in the body, we are abroad from the Lord." This indicates that to be at home in the body is to be abroad from the Lord and to be abroad from the body is to be at home with the Lord. Some may ask, "Does this not imply going to heaven?" This is their inference, but this is not what the Bible says. This matter of being at home with the Lord is a rather complicated matter. The proper explanation of 2 Corinthians 5:8 and Philippians 1:23 is as follows. When we are in the body, we are in the material world. The Lord, however, having resurrected and ascended, is in the spiritual world. We are in the material world, and the Lord is in the spiritual world. Hence, there is a physical barrier. When we die, our soul and spirit are separated from our body. Our soul and spirit then depart from the material world to go to the spiritual world.

In this sense we are closer to the Lord after we die because we are no longer in the material world but in the spiritual world, the same realm in which the Lord is. By this we can see that we are surely closer to the Lord when we are in the same realm as He is and in the same place as He is. Yet there are numerous other places in the spiritual realm besides the third heaven. For example, a few years ago a few saints came to be trained in Taipei. Some people said that those saints were with Brother Lee because Brother Lee was also in Taipei at that time. Geographically speaking, they were with Brother Lee in Taipei. However, those saints who had come to Taipei at that time realized that they were living in their own place while Brother Lee was living in his. Although they were all in Taipei, they were not living in the same room with Brother Lee. Brother Lee was living in his home while they were living in a co-workers' home. Although they and Brother Lee were living in the same city of Taipei, they were not living in the same place with Brother Lee. Similarly, when a saint dies, leaves his body, and departs from the material world, he goes to the spiritual world where the Lord is to be with Him. However, it is not so easy to explain where the Lord is in the spiritual world because the spiritual world includes not only the third heaven but also other places, one of which is the Paradise in Hades. This fully proves that to be abroad from the body and at home with the Lord is not to go to heaven.

THE THIRD HEAVEN AND PARADISE
BEING TWO DIFFERENT PLACES

People may then ask how we can explain 2 Corinthians 12. In verses 1 through 4 Paul says, "To boast is necessary, though indeed not expedient; yet I will come to visions and revelations of the Lord. I know a man in Christ, fourteen years ago (whether in the body I do not know, or outside the body I do not know; God knows) such a one was caught away to the third heaven. And I know such a man (whether in the body or outside the body, I do not know; God knows), that he was caught away into Paradise and heard unspeakable words, which it is not allowed for a man to speak." Many people say that since these verses mention the third heaven as well as Paradise, Paradise must be the third heaven. However, the word *and* at the beginning of verse 3 before the phrase *I know such a man* indicates that to be caught away to the third heaven in the preceding verse is one thing, and to be caught away into Paradise in the following verse is another.

In short, this man was brought to the third heaven as well as to Paradise. The third heaven and Paradise are two different places. Therefore, these verses do not prove that Paradise is in the third heaven. Rather, they prove that Paradise in Hades and the third heaven in the heavens are two different places. Paul said that God had given him the greatest revelations for him to understand all kinds of mysteries. He was a man on the earth and knew about almost everything on the earth. Therefore, God brought him to the third heaven to see the things in the third heaven, and he saw them. Yet in the universe there are not only the heavens and the earth but also Hades under the earth. Philippians 2 says that the Lord was exalted to the heavens that in the name of Jesus every knee would bow, "of those who are in heaven and on earth and under the earth, and every tongue should openly confess that Jesus Christ is Lord" (vv. 9-11). Hence, God also brought Paul to Paradise under the earth. In this way, Paul's revelation was completed. He was a man on the earth but had also been to the third heaven and to Paradise under the earth. Therefore,

Paul had seen all the things in heaven, on earth, and under the earth. This is what Paul meant.

Some may then ask why some translations of 2 Corinthians 12:4, including the Chinese Union Version, say "caught up into Paradise" if Paradise is under the earth. According to the Greek text, the literal translation should be *caught away*. To be caught up implies to go up from a place that is below, whereas to be caught away is to be brought away. Paul was caught away, brought away, and brought into Paradise. Thus, there is no problem in this case. These verses also do not prove that Paradise has been transferred to the third heaven. On the contrary, they prove that Paradise and the third heaven are two distinct places.

THE SPIRITS OF RIGHTEOUS MEN
WHO HAVE BEEN MADE PERFECT
NOT BEING IN A HEAVENLY MANSION

Some people may point to another portion of the Bible, Hebrews 12:18, which says, "For you have not come forward to a mountain which could be touched and which was set on fire." We all know that this mountain is Mount Sinai where the Israelites received the law in the Old Testament. Most Bible readers acknowledge that Mount Sinai represents Judaism, which is of the law. The Hebrew believers were previously in the Old Testament religion of Judaism and in a spiritual sense were at Mount Sinai. One day, they believed in the Lord and came out of the Old Testament age, out of Judaism. The apostle therefore wrote to them, saying that they had not come to Mount Sinai but "to Mount Zion and to the city of the living God, the heavenly Jerusalem" (v. 22).

Mount Zion denotes God's habitation in the heavens, that is, the center of the holy city Jerusalem. Most Bible readers acknowledge that in a spiritual sense Mount Sinai, which was mentioned earlier, represents the law and Judaism, and that Mount Zion represents the new covenant and grace. This means that the Hebrew believers had come under the new covenant, that is, into grace. This Mount Zion is the city of the living God, the heavenly Jerusalem.

Verses 22b to 24 continue, "And to myriads of angels, to

the universal gathering; and to the church of the firstborn, who have been enrolled in the heavens; and to God, the Judge of all; and to the spirits of righteous men who have been made perfect; and to Jesus, the Mediator of a new covenant; and to the blood of sprinkling." The word *and* is used seven times in verses 22 through 24 where eight items are mentioned. The first item is Mount Zion. The word *and* after *Mount Zion* indicates that "the city of the living God, the heavenly Jerusalem" is the second item. The "myriads of angels" is the third item, and "the church of the firstborn, who have been enrolled in the heavens" is the fourth item. However, do not think that this means that the church is in the heavens. The verse says that they have been enrolled in the heavens; it does not say that the church went to the heavens. The fifth item is "God, the Judge of all," and the sixth item is "the spirits of righteous men who have been made perfect." "Jesus, the Mediator of a new covenant" is the seventh item, and "the blood of sprinkling" is the eighth item.

First, there is Mount Zion; second, there is the city of the living God, that is, the heavenly Jerusalem; third, there are the angels; fourth, there is the church of the firstborn; fifth, there is God, the Judge of all; sixth, there are the spirits of righteous men who have been made perfect; seventh, there is the Mediator of a new covenant; and eighth, there is the blood of sprinkling. Thus, in these verses there are eight items with seven *and*s. One of the items is the spirits of the righteous men who have been made perfect. This refers to the spirits of the saved ones in the Old Testament. It may appear to some that the spirits of the righteous men are included in Mount Zion, that is, in the heavens. Apparently this is true, but actually it is not, because the church is also listed here and is included in these eight items. If the spirits of the righteous men who have been made perfect have gone to the heavens or to a heavenly mansion, then the church must have also gone to the heavens, to a heavenly mansion.

The book of Hebrews indicates that all the Hebrew believers had once been under the Old Testament law but had now come under grace in the New Testament. There are eight items with regard to grace, but although these eight items are heavenly, this does not mean that they are in the heavens. Concerning grace, Paul listed items such as Mount Zion, the heavenly Jerusalem, the myriads of angels, the church, and so forth. We all realize that the church is not something in the heavens. The church has not gone to the heavens. When Paul wrote the book of Hebrews, the church had not gone to the heavens. Similarly, the blood sprinkled by the Lord Jesus is not in the heavens in a physical sense; only its efficacy has reached the heavens. Therefore, in terms of their significance, these items are all heavenly, but physically speaking, they are not in the heavens. Therefore, how can one say that the spirits of those saved in the Old Testament are in the heavens?

THE SPIRIT OF STEPHEN
BEING IN PARADISE UNDER THE EARTH

At the end of Acts 7 Stephen was martyred, and while he was being stoned, he said, "Lord Jesus, receive my spirit!" (v. 59). Some use this to say that Stephen's spirit went to a heavenly mansion. They think that since the Lord is in heaven, when He received Stephen's spirit He must have received it into heaven. Again, this is an inference. This is not the truth. Suppose I give something to someone. After he receives it, he may not necessarily put it beside him or bring it to his room. He could put it in another place. The Lord Jesus undoubtedly received the spirit of Stephen, but we cannot arbitrarily say that He received it in the third heaven where He is.

Ecclesiastes 3:21 says, "Who knows the breath of the children of men, that it goes upward; or the breath of the beasts, that it goes downward to the earth?" Some translate the word *breath* in this verse as *spirit* in the first instance and *soul* in the second. Based upon this, some conclude that this verse states that the spirits of the saved ones go upward and the souls of the beasts go downward to the earth. However, this is again a problem in translation. The Hebrew word used in this verse should be translated *spirit* or *breath*. Ecclesiastes talks about everything being vanity of vanities (1:2). Then in chapter three it goes on to say that there is not much difference

between men and beasts (vv. 18-20). This is what the writer
of Ecclesiastes meant. Therefore, when he comes to verse 21
he asks, "Who knows the breath of the children of men?"
meaning, "Who understands the breath of men?" This is a
question. We can also put another question mark after the
next phrase—*that it goes upward.* Furthermore, the verse
ends with the phrase *the breath of the beasts, that it goes
downward.* The question mark at the end of this phrase indicates that this is a question as well, meaning, "Does the
breath of the beasts go downward?" This verse does not conclude that the spirits of men go upward and that the souls of
beasts go downward. It merely shows us that no one can
understand where the breath of man goes—upward or otherwise. Whether it is upward or otherwise, it is vanity of vanities
and is not worth considering.

Many people also refer to Ecclesiastes 12:7, which says, "And
the dust returns to the earth as it was, and the breath returns
to God who gave it." They say that the body dies and returns to
the earth and that the spirit returns to God who gave it. Since
God is in heaven, they conclude that the spirit must go to a
heavenly mansion. This again is an inference. We have already
said that although the Lord Jesus receives the spirits and
souls of the believers, He does not necessarily place them in a
heavenly mansion. For example, when I return money to you
and you receive it, instead of putting it in your pocket, you may
deposit it in the bank. Ecclesiastes 12:7 indicates that the body
comes out of the earth and naturally returns to the earth.
However, since the spirit and soul are given by God, when the
believers die, their spirits and souls cannot remain in the
material world and must therefore return to God's spiritual
world. Although they return to God, there are particular
details in regard to how He arranges for them and where He
puts them.

The passages quoted above are all from the Old Testament. We can also use the Old Testament saints as examples
to illustrate that the spirits and souls of the dead believers
went to Sheol. The spirits and souls of people like Abraham,
Isaac, and Jacob indeed returned to God, but Genesis clearly
tells us that their spirits and souls are in Sheol.

BEING CLOTHED WITH THE GLORIFIED BODY
IN RESURRECTION

The spirit and soul of a person are the person himself, and a person's body is like his clothing, which is clearly shown in 2 Corinthians 5. Man's spirit and soul are clothed with the body, without which man is naked. If someone today came into our midst unclothed, I believe we would not even dare to look at him. We may even wonder if this person had become insane and abnormal. We all love the apostle Paul, but if Paul's spirit and soul were here without his body, would we dare to shake hands with him? I am afraid we would all be scared away. We would be scared because he would be in an abnormal condition. When a believer dies, his spirit and soul are separated from his body, and death is written all over him. Death is even filthier than sin. Nothing of death can be brought before God because God is the God of the living, not of the dead. Every dead person must wait until resurrection when his spirit and soul will be properly clothed with the body before he can come to God.

The Old Testament explicitly says that when a person came to serve God in the Holy Place, he had to be properly dressed. He could not be naked or have any condition of death upon him (cf. Exo. 28:40-43), because death could not be brought into God's dwelling place. When those who have been saved die, they also cannot go to God's dwelling place in the heavens. God therefore puts their spirits and souls in the Paradise in Hades so that they may rest and wait there. What are they waiting for? They are waiting for the resurrection. Once they are resurrected, their spirits and souls will be clothed with their bodies, and death will be swallowed up. Thus, their naked condition will also be gone. At that time they will be clothed with glorified bodies to enter properly and appropriately into God's dwelling place, that is, God's eternal kingdom.

CHAPTER TWO

THE SAVED ONES RECEIVING
THE PROMISE OF GOD IN FULL
IN THE NEW JERUSALEM

AFTER DEATH THE BELIEVERS NOT GOING
TO THE THIRD HEAVEN WHERE GOD DWELLS

When people speak of heaven and Hades, they often base their speaking on verses that are inaccurately used. Many people say that after the Lord ascended to heaven, the Paradise of Hades was also moved to heaven. Based upon this, they conclude that ever since the Lord's death and resurrection, the souls and spirits of dead believers also go to heaven. In the previous message we studied almost all the verses that these ones use as their basis. As a result, we found that not one of these verses clearly states that the souls and spirits of dead believers go to heaven. We saw that this argument is based merely on inferences. Therefore, we must continue to search the Scriptures to see where the spirits and souls of dead believers go.

John 3:13, which was spoken by the Lord Jesus while He was on the earth as the Son of Man, says, "And no one has ascended into heaven, but He who descended out of heaven, the Son of Man, who is in heaven." While the Lord was on the earth, He said that no one had ascended to heaven. This indicates that all the spirits and souls of the saints who died in the Old Testament did not go to heaven, because no one other than the Lord had ever ascended to heaven. These words prove that the concept commonly held by many people concerning heaven is incorrect. Some people may point out that Enoch and Elijah were taken by God and that they must have been taken to heaven where God dwells. But the Lord's words in

John 3 prove that such an inference is not accurate. Enoch and Elijah were taken by God from the earth, but where God put them is not for us to know.

From John 3:13 we can see that God did not put the spirits and souls of these two men in the place where He dwells. We have already said that God's dwelling place is the third heaven. The Lord said in verse 13 that no one has ascended into heaven. *Heaven* in this verse refers to the third heaven where God dwells, because that is the place that the Lord descended from. Since this is the heaven from which the Lord descended, this is also the heaven where God dwells. The Lord said that up to that point no one had entered into heaven. This tells us that neither Enoch nor Elijah ascended to heaven.

BELIEVERS GOING TO HADES AFTER DEATH

If this is true, then where did God put them? If they were not put in the third heaven where God dwells, where else could they have been put? The Lord clearly said that no one other than the Son of Man had ever ascended into heaven. This indicates that Enoch and Elijah never went to the third heaven where God dwells. This amply proves that there must be another place besides the third heaven where God is. It is in this other place that God must have placed Enoch and Elijah. In any case, the Bible clearly indicates that they were not put in the third heaven where God dwells.

Acts 2:31 through 32 speaks of the resurrection of the Lord Jesus. This was prophesied in Psalm 16, one of David's psalms, which prophesied that after the Lord went to Hades, God would cause Him to rise and come out of Hades. Acts 2:31 says that David, "seeing this beforehand, spoke concerning the resurrection of the Christ, that neither was He abandoned to Hades, nor did His flesh see corruption." There are two points of significance here. First, the Lord must have descended to Hades, because if He had not, it would have been unnecessary to say that He would not be abandoned to Hades. Second, in His resurrection the Lord must have come out of Hades. Only by coming out of Hades could the word concerning His not being abandoned to Hades be fulfilled.

In Psalm 16 David prophesied that the Lord's body would not see corruption after death. This was a proof that the Lord would be resurrected soon after His death. If He had been raised after three months or one year, His body would have been corrupted. Instead, only three days after His death He was resurrected. Therefore, His body did not see corruption. Acts 2:32 says, "This Jesus God has raised up." From the context we can see that the resurrection includes the spirit and soul coming out from Hades and the body coming out from the tomb. After the Lord Jesus resurrected, He ascended to heaven. From John 3 we can clearly see that at the time the Lord was on the earth no one had ascended to heaven. Only after the Lord Jesus resurrected could one say that a man had ascended to heaven, and that man was Jesus the Nazarene.

TWO PARTS OF HADES

In the Scofield Reference Bible there is a footnote for Luke 16:23 regarding Hades. This footnote says that before the Lord Jesus ascended, Hades had two parts. One part was the place for the spirits and souls of the unsaved people. This is the place of torment where the rich man was. The second part was the place for the spirits and souls of the saved ones, which the Lord Jesus called Paradise in speaking to the thief on the cross and which was also the place where Lazarus was in the bosom of Abraham. This explanation by Scofield is biblical and correct. There is no problem with this explanation.

According to what we have seen, Hades definitely has two parts. One part is the place of flames where the rich man was, and the other is the place of comfort and joy where Lazarus was in the bosom of Abraham. Luke also calls this place Paradise, the place where the spirits and souls of the saved ones in past generations are resting. This is very much in accordance with the Bible. However, Mr. Scofield clearly emphasizes that after the Lord Jesus' resurrection and ascension, there was a change related to the Paradise of Hades. He said that when the Lord Jesus ascended, He brought Paradise, along with the spirits and souls of the saved saints in the Old Testament, to heaven. In other words, Mr. Scofield believed that when the Lord ascended, He also transferred the Paradise of Hades with the spirits and souls that were in it to the third heaven. He even uses the Paradise mentioned in 2 Corinthians 12:4 to indicate that Paradise was moved to the third heaven. We have already seen in the previous message that 2 Corinthians 12 does not prove that Paradise is in the third heaven. On the contrary, it shows us that Paradise and the third heaven are two different places. When the Lord Jesus resurrected and ascended, the Paradise of Hades did not move to a different place. Paradise is still in Hades, and the spirits and souls of the Old Testament saints are still in the Paradise of Hades waiting for resurrection.

THE LORD JESUS ALONE
HAVING RESURRECTED AND ASCENDED

Acts 2:34 says, "David did not ascend into the heavens." These words were spoken by Peter on the day of Pentecost after the Lord Jesus had ascended. Mr. Scofield says that when the Lord Jesus ascended to the heavens, He brought with Him the saved souls and spirits of the Old Testament saints. We believe that David is among the saved souls and spirits of the Old Testament saints. Then, according to Mr. Scofield's view, on the day of Pentecost David should have been in heaven. But on the day of Pentecost, Peter, having been inspired by the Holy Spirit, stood up and said, "David did not ascend into the heavens." Mr. Scofield says that when the Lord Jesus ascended to the heavens, David also ascended. But on the day of Pentecost, Peter said that David did not ascend into the heavens. David prophesied that when Christ resurrected and ascended to the heavens, He would sit on the right hand of God. According to Acts 2, after the Lord Jesus resurrected and ascended, the souls and spirits of the Old Testament saints did not ascend to the heavens. Only the Lord Jesus Himself resurrected and ascended. This is very clear.

We must always remember Acts 2:34, which says, "David did not ascend into the heavens." If anyone tells us that the Lord Jesus brought the souls and spirits of the Old Testament saints to the heavens in His ascension, we can read Acts 2:34 to him and tell him, "David did not ascend into the heavens."

Then we can read Hebrews 11:10, which says that Abraham waited for the city with foundations, whose Architect and Builder is God. Verse 16 says, "They long after a better country, that is, a heavenly one. Therefore God is not ashamed of them, to be called their God, for He has prepared a city for them." Most Bible readers agree that what Abraham waited for was the city God had promised him—the heavenly New Jerusalem.

Abraham still longs for the heavenly city, which is the New Jerusalem. In the previous message we saw that after their death the souls and spirits of Abraham, Isaac, and Jacob went to Hades, not to heaven. Therefore, when the Lord was on the earth, He said that no one had ascended into heaven. On the day of Pentecost in Acts 2, Peter also said that David did not ascend to the heavens. If what Mr. Scofield believed is right, then in Hebrews, Abraham should have already been in the holy city, the Jerusalem in the heavens. Mr. Scofield said that when Christ resurrected and ascended, He transferred the spirits and souls of the Old Testament saints to the heavens. Mr. Scofield believed that the Lord brought them into the heavens, into the New Jerusalem. Consequently, Abraham should have already obtained the city that he longs for and that God has promised him. However, Hebrews 11:39 says, "And these all, having obtained a good testimony through their faith, did not obtain the promise."

ALL THE BELIEVERS ENTERING
INTO THE NEW JERUSALEM TOGETHER

Hebrews 11 was written with a single line of thought. It speaks of many who believed in and hoped to obtain God's promise. This group of people, mentioned in verses 2 through 38, includes Abraham. What happened to Abraham and these men? Through faith they all received a good testimony, but they did not obtain the promise. Did Abraham obtain the holy city New Jerusalem that he longed for? Did Abraham receive the city that God had promised him? Verse 39 says very clearly that these ones did not obtain God's promise. Today Abraham is still hoping and waiting in Paradise in Hades. When will he receive the city God promised him? Verse 40 says, "Because God has provided something better for us, so that apart from us they would not be made perfect."

This is the word of the Bible. Abraham will not enter into the city before us. He is waiting for us in Paradise. The Paradise of Hades is where those who have been saved go after death. As each one dies, each one enters into it. On the other hand, the holy city New Jerusalem is not a place that we enter one by one but a place that we enter in a corporate way. The Old Testament saints could not enter into the holy city immediately after their death. They must wait for the New Testament saints. All those who know the Bible and have read Hebrews 11 recognize that although the Old Testament saints were saved before us, they cannot enter into the New Jerusalem earlier than we do. God wants them to wait for us who are in the New Testament age.

Strictly speaking, God has not finished His work on Abraham, Isaac, and Jacob. How can we say this? We can say this because Abraham, Isaac, and Jacob have not resurrected, that is, their bodies are still in the tomb. God's work with regard to their bodies has not yet been completed. They are dead people. Regardless of how much they loved the Lord or how spiritual they may have been, they are still under death. Death is still in their bodies. When will this problem of death be resolved? This problem will be resolved when God finishes His work in all the saints throughout the ages and generations. When God causes the Lord Jesus to return, and when all the dead saints are resurrected, then the work of God on Abraham, Isaac, and Jacob will be finished. At the same time, the work of God in us will also be completed. In other words, when they and we are resurrected, God's work on them and on us will be completed. They and we, we and they, will enter into the New Jerusalem together and at the same time.

Today when a saint dies, there is still one problem that remains unresolved—the problem of death. Before this problem is solved, God places these spirits and souls in the Paradise of Hades. This Paradise is not the eternal dwelling place of those who have been saved. It is only a temporary shelter for the spirits and souls of the saved ones after they die and before they enter into the New Jerusalem. Therefore, today Abraham is still in the Paradise of Hades and has not entered into the holy city that he longed for. He is still in Paradise, waiting for what God promised him. According to God's ordination, the Old Testament saints and the New Testament saints are to enter into the New Jerusalem together. This is what the Lord clearly revealed in Hebrews 11.

According to God's plan and arrangement, when a saint dies, his spirit and soul do not go into the holy city New Jerusalem but into the Paradise of Hades. God's plan has not been fulfilled yet, His preparation has not been completed yet, the time has not yet come, the required number of saints has not yet been reached, and God's work in the saints has not yet been fully accomplished. Therefore, there must be a period of waiting with patience. Thus, God temporarily keeps the dead saints' spirits and souls in Paradise where they must wait. From Hebrews 11 we can see that Abraham, Jacob, Joseph, and Moses are all there. Of course, if we read Matthew 17, we can see that there is another arrangement for Moses and Elijah. In God's plan and work there are many arrangements and considerations. It is not as simple as we may think. Nevertheless, until the day of resurrection arrives, the spirits and souls of the dead saints will be temporarily kept in Paradise. No one can enter into the New Jerusalem before the appointed time or before all the requirements are met.

THE SAVED ONES NEEDING TO BE COMPLETE AND WITHOUT ANY PROBLEMS TO ENTER INTO THE HOLY CITY

In Matthew 27, when the Lord Jesus resurrected, there were some Old Testament saints who came out of the tombs, entered into the earthly city of Jerusalem, and appeared to many people (vv. 52-53). Where did those dead saints go after they resurrected? We can only say that we do not know because the New Testament does not clearly tell us this, and we do not want to assume too much. However, the day of Christ's resurrection is typified by the Feast of the Firstfruits (Lev. 23:10), because the Feast of the Firstfruits was fifty days prior to the day of Pentecost, and it was on this day that the Holy Spirit descended in Acts 2. In the Old Testament

during the Feast of the Firstfruits, God required the Israelites to offer a sheaf of the firstfruits of their produce. The
produce that was offered was a sheaf, not merely one stalk. If
the offering had been only one stalk, then this would have
indicated that the Lord Jesus was going to be resurrected
alone. However, the fact that the offering was a sheaf of
firstfruits, indicated that besides the Lord Jesus, the saints
who came out from the tombs in Matthew 27 would also be
resurrected. They became the firstfruits of the harvest along
with the Lord Jesus. However, where God placed them after
they resurrected is difficult to determine from the Word, and
we dare not draw any conclusions.

In simple terms, in order for a saved one to enter into
God's dwelling place, he must be mature, and he must be a
complete person with his spirit, soul, and body in resurrection. He cannot be one whose spirit and soul have been
separated from the body and whose body has not yet been resurrected. The spirit and soul of a dead person must be clothed
with the body in resurrection to form a complete person. Only
such a complete person is qualified to come before God's presence. Even when the Lord Jesus died, His spirit and soul did
not go directly to heaven. His spirit and soul went to the Paradise of Hades first. Only on the day of resurrection, after His
spirit and soul had put on His body again, did He ascend to
heaven to meet God.

Do you think that after the saints die, they can immediately go to heaven to meet God in a state of nakedness,
without resurrecting and putting on the body? Suppose that
today Paul's spirit and soul came to visit us. If he had no body
and only his spirit and soul came to us, would we not be
frightened? The spirit and soul without the body is like a
person without any clothing.

Second Corinthians 5 clearly says that the body is like our
clothing (vv. 1-4). Not only will we be unclothed of this body,
but we will eventually be clothed with a transfigured body.
Paul says that if we are clothed with that body, we will not be
found naked when we meet God. In other words, suppose we
are unclothed of this body, that is, we die. If we meet God
without being clothed with a transfigured body, that is, if we

are not yet resurrected, we will be naked. This is what the apostle means. No matter how many times we read 2 Corinthians 5, it will always have this meaning. First, we cannot meet God in this body of humiliation. Second, even if we were unclothed of this body of humiliation, we still would not be able to meet God because we would be naked. Only when we are clothed with that body—the resurrected, transfigured, and glorified body—will we no longer be naked. Then we will be able to meet God.

This shows us a principle. For a person who has been saved to go to God in the heavens and to be with God, he must be complete and without any problems. If a saved person dies, and his spirit and soul leave his body, there is still the problem of death in him. As long as this problem of death is not solved, his spirit and soul are still naked. How can such a person go to the dwelling place of God and dwell with Him? Therefore, he must be temporarily placed in the Paradise of Hades to wait there. As an illustration, suppose we come to visit you as you are taking a bath. At such a time, surely you would want us to wait outside until you finished taking your bath in the bathroom, put on some clothes, and could come out to the living room to meet us. If you heard us come and immediately came out from your bathroom without putting on any clothes, we would run away in fright. We must wait until you put on your clothes before we can meet you.

THE THOUGHT IN THE BIBLE
REGARDING MAN'S FINAL END

The thought in the Bible is that God has definitely ordained that those who have been saved would enter into the "living room," but they must first be properly clothed and complete. When a saint dies, before the time of rapture and resurrection, his spirit and soul leaves his body and becomes naked, having the condition of death. A big mark of death, the fact of death, is on him. Do you think that God would let such a naked spirit and soul, bearing a big mark of death, go to the heavens where His dwelling place is to be with Him? Of course He would not allow this. So what does God do? God does have a heart's desire for those who are saved, who mature, and who die early. God seems to tell such a one, "You have had enough suffering, trials, and pains on the earth. Now I will put your spirit and soul in the bosom of Abraham. There you can rest, be comforted, and wait in peace until I finish My work. I still need to work in many people. You must wait until My work is finished, the days are fulfilled, and all the requirements are met. On that day when the holy city New Jerusalem is manifested, all the spirits and souls of those who have been saved throughout the generations will put on resurrected, transformed, and glorified bodies. You will be properly clothed and complete, and you will live with Me in the eternal dwelling place." This is the thought of the Bible.

THE DEAD BELIEVERS RESTING AND WAITING
IN THE PARADISE OF HADES

However, there is another problem—where are the spirits and souls of the dead believers? Revelation 6:9 says, "And when He opened the fifth seal, I saw underneath the altar the souls of those who had been slain because of the word of God and because of the testimony which they had." The opening of the fifth seal is closely followed by the opening of the sixth seal and is very close to the end of this age. In the sixth seal the heaven and earth and the moon and the sun are changed. So the fifth seal is close to the end of this age. The souls of those who were slain include the Old Testament and New Testament martyrs, including Peter and Paul. These souls "cried with a loud voice, saying, How long, O Master, holy and true, will You not judge and avenge our blood on those who dwell on the earth? And to each of them was given a white robe; and it was said to them that they should rest yet a little while" (vv. 10-11). This word *rest* is a good translation. It proves that the souls of the martyred saints are being comforted and are resting a little while in the bosom of Abraham. The words *a little while* also prove that the end of this age is near.

Where are the souls of the martyred saints, those whom the Lord wants to rest a little while? They are under the altar. This altar is typified in the Old Testament. According to the

Old Testament type, the altar was in the outer court, not in the Holy Place or in the Holy of Holies. Most Bible readers acknowledge that the Holy of Holies typifies heaven, the outer court typifies earth, and the activity at the altar typifies something that was accomplished on the earth. The altar in the Old Testament typifies the cross in the New Testament. The cross was not in the heavens but was erected on the earth, on top of a mountain outside Jerusalem. This tells us that the altar is something earthly. Then what does it mean to be underneath the altar? To be underneath the altar is to be underneath the earth.

The souls of the martyred saints are crying from underneath the altar, from the Paradise of Hades, which is underneath the earth. The souls of the martyred saints did not ascend to heaven at the time of the Lord Jesus' ascension. Even at the opening of the fifth seal when the Lord's return is imminent, their souls will still be underneath the altar in the Paradise of Hades. If they were already in heaven and in the holy city, they would not cry aloud. However, because they have not obtained what they hoped for and believed in, they are desperate. So the Lord tells them that they must rest a little while. This clearly shows us that the souls of all the saints who died for the Lord in the Old Testament and the New Testament are underneath the altar, that is, underneath the earth in the Paradise of Hades, enjoying rest.

First Corinthians 3:15 says, "He himself will be saved, yet so as through fire." Catholicism teaches the concept of purgatory based on this verse. We can only say that this concept is absolutely inaccurate. Protestantism also incorrectly teaches that all the dead saints go to heaven. These are two erroneous teachings. Catholicism says that the spirits and souls of the dead go to purgatory to suffer, and Protestantism says that the spirits and souls of the dead go to heaven to enjoy eternal bliss. Both concepts are erroneous. According to the truth in the Bible, it does not matter whether a person who has been saved is strong or weak. As long as he has believed in the Lord's saving precious blood, his spirit and soul will go to the Paradise in Hades when he dies.

WAITING IN PARADISE FOR RESURRECTION AND FOR THE RESOLUTION OF THE ISSUES OF DEATH, MATURITY, AND JUDGMENT

What are the saints doing in the Paradise of Hades? They are waiting for resurrection, because the issues of death and maturity in life must be resolved. They are not suffering in Paradise but are resting and waiting. They are waiting for the resurrection and for the issue of the maturity in life to be resolved. They are waiting to receive either reward or punishment before the judgment seat of Christ. Once a believer dies, his spirit and soul go to rest in Paradise. However, this does not mean that there are no more problems. There are at least three issues that must be resolved: resurrection, maturity in life, and the receiving of either reward or punishment before the judgment seat of Christ. Only after these issues are resolved can a believer enter into God's dwelling place in completeness and without problems.

Today when someone dies, there is nothing that can be done about his death. If he is a saved person, he does not go into the flames of Hades because his sins have been borne by the Lord. He does not suffer by the fire. However, there are still some issues that remain unresolved. Death is an issue that still needs to be resolved because the resurrection has not occurred yet. Furthermore, there are the issues of the maturity in life and the receiving of either reward or punishment according to the Lord's judgment. Therefore, the saved one must wait in the Paradise of Hades for the resurrection and for the resolving of the issues of the maturity in life and for the receiving of either reward or punishment before the judgment seat of Christ.

After these problems are solved, he will be a complete person. Then God's work in him will be finished. On that day God will place him in His dwelling place. The teaching of Protestantism that a Christian goes to heaven after death is not according to the truth. After a Christian dies, he still has the problem of death and still needs to be resurrected. He also needs to pass through the judgment at the judgment seat of Christ to decide whether he will receive reward or punishment. After going through all these processes and resolving all these issues, he will finally be a complete person before God. The work of God in him will finally be considered complete. On that day the holy city New Jerusalem will finally be prepared and ready. Also on that day the people who will enter the holy city and enjoy the eternal blessing will be satisfied. At that time all those who have been saved will finally receive what they believed in and hoped for throughout the generations. They will receive what God promised them throughout the generations.

Before that day arrives, the dead saints are in an abnormal situation of having their spirits and souls separated from their bodies. Thus, they need to be temporarily placed in Paradise to rest and to wait for the resurrection and for their being clothed with a glorious body. At the same time, we still may not be conformed to Christ's image, we may not be mature in life, and we may not be faithful to God and may still have a big problem in serving Him. All these matters need to be taken care of in the future. When all these issues are resolved, then God's work on us will finally be finished. Only then will the New Jerusalem be manifested, and God and we will dwell together eternally.

CHAPTER THREE

THE THREE PARADISES
FOR THREE PERIODS OF TIME

Scripture Readings: Gen. 2:8, 9b-12; Rev. 21:1a, 2-3, 10-11, 18-19a, 21; 22:1-2

In the last message we saw that the spirits and souls of dead believers did not ascend to heaven even after the Lord Jesus resurrected and ascended to heaven. Revelation 6:9 clearly says that at the time of the opening of the fifth seal, which occurs very close to the second coming of the Lord, the souls of the martyrs will still be underneath the altar, that is, in the Paradise of Hades. In this message we need to see in principle what the distinctive features of the heavenly New Jerusalem and the Paradise in Hades are. We have to see the consistent line in the Bible.

GOD'S PREPARATION OF A DWELLING PLACE FOR MAN

Most Bible readers acknowledge that at the beginning of the Bible in the book of Genesis God prepared a dwelling place for man (2:8). At the end of the Bible in Revelation we also see that God prepares a dwelling place for man (21:2). From beginning to end, the Bible is a record of God's preparation of a dwelling place for man.

THE TWO PARADISES—
THE GARDEN OF EDEN AND THE NEW JERUSALEM

The dwelling place God prepared for man in the beginning was called the garden of Eden, and the one at the end is called the New Jerusalem. *Eden* means "pleasure." Therefore, the garden of Eden was a paradise. The dwelling place at the end of the Bible—the New Jerusalem, which is mentioned at the beginning of Revelation 2—is also a paradise. The paradise in Genesis 2 has the tree of life in it. Revelation 22 shows us that the New Jerusalem also has the tree of life in it. Thus, the paradise in Genesis 2 is the New Jerusalem in Revelation 22.

Here we see that the dwelling place God prepared for man in the beginning was a paradise and that the dwelling place God prepares for man in the end is also a paradise. Both are pleasant places, and their contents are also similar. The two paradises both have the tree of life and a river, and both have pure gold, pearl, and precious stones. This shows us that the dwelling place God prepared for man in the beginning is the same as the one He prepares for man at the end. The two places have almost the same contents. This tells us that what God did in the beginning was related to His ultimate purpose, and God's ultimate purpose is revealed in what He did in the beginning.

GOD'S PURPOSE BEING TO WORK HIMSELF INTO MAN

The two paradises in Genesis and Revelation are both dwelling places for man. They show us the purpose and reason why God prepared them for man. Our simple minds may think that God only wants us to go to heaven. However, God's thought is very different from ours. God's unique purpose in this universe is to work Himself into man so that man may have His life and nature and that through His life and nature, man may be transformed inwardly (2 Pet. 1:3-4; 2 Cor. 3:18). Ultimately, God and man will be mingled together, and man will have the image of God (Rom. 8:29). The inward being of God will be the inward being of man, and God's glorious, outward appearance will be man's glorious appearance (cf. Rev. 4:3; 21:11). As a result, God and man will be exactly the same both outwardly and inwardly.

In typology, pure gold is used to signify God's life and nature. Most Bible readers know that pure gold signifies God's life and nature. For example, the ark in the Old Testament tabernacle was overlaid with pure gold (Exo. 37:1-2). The lampstand was made of beaten work from one piece of pure gold (v. 17). Pure gold typifies the divine life and nature of the Lord Jesus.

The outward expression of God is usually symbolized by precious stones. In Exodus, when Moses saw God, he saw something like sapphire under His feet (24:10). When Daniel saw the Lord, the Lord looked like beryl (Dan. 10:6). In Revelation, John saw in a vision One who was sitting on the throne in heaven who was like a jasper stone and a sardius stone in appearance (4:3). There is no question that in the Bible precious stones signify the expression of the glorious image of God. I hope we all would remember the significance of the pure gold and the precious stones. The pure gold is God's life and nature, and the precious stones are the expression of God's glorious image.

Pure gold signifies God's nature, and precious stones signify His glory. God's purpose is to work in us to the extent that we become exactly the same as He is. He wants to put His nature into us so that we may be transformed to the point of having His image outwardly. Do we have the pure gold and the precious stones? The pure gold is God's nature, and the precious stones are God's glorious image. Do we who are under the work of God's grace have the pure gold and the precious stones? The pure gold signifies God's life and nature, which is inward, whereas the precious stones signify God's glorious image, which is expressed outwardly. Since we all have been saved by grace, we at least have the pure gold, which is God's life and nature.

Peter tells us that God has given us His life so that we can be partakers of His nature (2 Pet. 1:3-4). Once we are saved, God's life with His nature enters into us; thus, we have the pure gold in us. However, we may not have the precious stones outwardly. In other words, our outward man may be the same and may not have changed much. For example, before some saints were saved, they were not only created human beings but human beings who had become a mess. One day, however, they were saved and were cleansed by the Lord. They received the Lord's life and nature and became clean within. Yet outwardly, they are still the same. They are still what they were by creation without any outward change. In other words, they do not express the glorious image of God. They are still what they were originally, except that they do not sin as they did before. Hence, in their outward being they are still the original old man. Is this old man made of precious stones or clay? Our old man is a "clay man." One gets dirty simply by touching this clay man.

GOD WANTING TO TRANSFORM THE MAN OF CLAY INTO PURE GOLD AND PRECIOUS STONES

Genesis 2:7 records that in the beginning God formed man with the dust of the ground, 1 Corinthians 15:47 tells us that Adam is earthy, and 2 Corinthians 4:7 says that we were created to be earthen vessels. The term *earthen vessel* in Greek denotes an earthy vessel made of clay. Hence, even after receiving the life and nature of the pure gold within, we still may not have the image of the precious stones without. We may still be earthy. We remain the same because the life of God has not yet transformed us enough.

After we are saved, although we may not sin as we did before, much of our being remains unchanged. Even though we may be somewhat transformed into the image of Christ, that amount of transformation is not enough. We have the life and nature of the pure gold within, but we may be short of the glorious image of the precious stones without. When God first put Adam in the garden of Eden, there were pure gold and precious stones there. God's purpose was that the man of clay would be transformed into pure gold and precious stone. Therefore, in the garden of Eden we can see the tree of life and the river of life. God wanted Adam to receive the life from the tree of life and the river of life so that he could be transformed into pure gold and precious stone.

THE NEW JERUSALEM BEING BOTH A CITY AND A PERSON

When we come to Revelation 21, a city of pure gold appears, and a wall of precious stones is manifested. The street of this city is pure gold, and the outward wall is composed of precious stones. This city is a sign with a twofold significance. On one hand, this city signifies a place, because it is a city. On the other hand, it signifies a person because it is a bride, the wife of the Lamb. In other words, this city is the dwelling place of

God and all the saints, and it is also the issue of God's work in man throughout the ages. This city is a man of glory. In the garden of Eden in Genesis, we see man, pure gold, and precious stones. The man, the pure gold, and the precious stones are separate from each other. When we come to the New Jerusalem in Revelation 21, we see pure gold and precious stones but no man. Where is man? Can anyone find man in the New Jerusalem in Revelation 21? In Genesis we can see man in the garden of Eden, but in Revelation we cannot see man in the New Jerusalem. Why is this? This is because the New Jerusalem in Revelation 21 is the issue of God's work in man throughout the ages. The city, the place itself is man. In the New Jerusalem, man, the pure gold, and the precious stones are one and cannot be separated.

On the foundations of the wall of the city we can see the names of the twelve apostles, but we cannot see the twelve apostles themselves. In this respect the New Jerusalem is different from the garden of Eden. In the garden of Eden we can see Adam and Eve. However, if we went to the city in Revelation and saw a stone with Peter's name on it and asked where Peter was, I am afraid Peter would tell us, "I am actually this stone." This is not our own inference. In 1 Peter 2, Peter says that every saved one is a living stone before the Lord and is being built together with the Lord Jesus to be a spiritual house for God's dwelling (v. 5). In Ephesians 2 Paul also says that the saved ones are "being built upon the foundation of the apostles and prophets, Christ Jesus Himself being the cornerstone; in whom all the building, being fitted together, is growing into a holy temple in the Lord" (vv. 20-21). In the Old Testament God's people were in the holy temple, but in the New Testament God's people are the holy temple. In the New Testament the physical temple is gone, and the saved ones are built together. In the New Testament the saved ones are the holy temple. Hence, we may say that the holy temple is a place and also a person.

Today the church has a twofold significance. On one hand it is a dwelling place, and on the other hand it is a group of people saved by God. In the same way, the coming New Jerusalem also has a twofold significance. On one hand it is God's dwelling place, a city, and on the other hand it is also God's counterpart, a bride. Therefore, in the New Jerusalem one stone is Peter, one stone is James, and another stone is John. The twelve precious stones, which are the foundations of the wall of the city, are the twelve apostles. All the saved ones throughout the ages are living stones. They all have the life of God in them, and in this life they are joined together to become the living dwelling place of God, a living city. This is the coming New Jerusalem.

People may ask why this city is also a bride. They may ask why it is both the dwelling place of God and also the wife of God. For example, when a man gets married, his bride is one thing—a person—and his bridal chamber is another thing—a building. But when God marries man, the bride and the bridal chamber will be one. The bridal chamber will be the bride, and the bride will be the bridal chamber. We cannot comprehend this in our mind. This is like Revelation 21, which says, "The street of the city was pure gold, like transparent glass" (v. 21). How can gold be transparent as glass? We cannot comprehend this. Nevertheless, we have to believe that this is not our interpretation but the revelation from the Bible. What God has been doing throughout the ages is transforming the redeemed ones with His life to make them precious stones. One day this group of people will fully become God's eternal dwelling place in the universe.

If you still want to go to "heaven," you will ultimately be disappointed. One day you will become the place that you want to go to. As the bride, do you merely wish to live in the bridal chamber? One day you will actually be the bridal chamber, because the bride of Christ is also His bridal chamber. This is indeed a mysterious and wonderful matter. Throughout the ages, God has been working continuously. Ultimately, He will make Himself one with man and bring heaven and earth together.

Christianity talks about the saved ones going up to heaven, but Revelation tells us that the coming New Jerusalem will come down out of heaven from God. We do not need to go up to the New Jerusalem because we are entering into it. In fact, we are not even merely entering into it. Instead, we are becoming part of the New Jerusalem. This is the result of God's mysterious plan throughout the ages. What are the new heaven and new earth, and what is the New Jerusalem? They are is the oneness of God and man and the oneness of heaven and earth with nothing in between.

HEAVEN AND EARTH, GOD AND MAN, BEING MINGLED INTO ONE

Currently, heaven and earth are widely separated by the air in between them. The air is the dwelling place of Satan (Eph. 2:2). As those who are on the earth, we love God and work with God who is in heaven. The more we work together, the closer we become. We will work together until one day Satan, who is between God and us, will be squeezed out. Where will Satan be then? He will be squeezed out into the lake of fire. On that day, we on earth who belong to God will not go up to heaven. Rather, the eternal dwelling place that God is preparing for us will come down out of heaven. When the new heaven, the new earth, and the New Jerusalem are manifested, it will not only be something glorious but also mysterious. God and man will be completely mingled together. Heaven and earth will also be fully joined together. God and man will be inseparable, and there will be no more distance between heaven and earth. In that day heaven, earth, God, and man will be completely mingled together into one.

Just as it is hard for us to comprehend pure gold that is transparent, it is also hard for us to comprehend this concept. Nevertheless, the Bible tells us that this is so. In the new heaven and new earth when the New Jerusalem is manifested, God and man will be completely mingled together, and heaven and the earth will also be fully joined together as one. This is the New Jerusalem, the dwelling place of God in man. Furthermore, this will be the eternal dwelling place of God and man. At that time, the whole composition of the New Jerusalem will simply be God Himself.

THE GARDEN OF EDEN BECOMING THE NEW JERUSALEM

The content of God is pure gold, and the expression of God

is precious stone. The street of the New Jerusalem is pure gold, and the foundations of the wall as its expression are adorned with every precious stone. The glory of the city is the same in appearance as the One sitting on the throne. They are both like jasper stone. At the beginning in Genesis, God started His work. What kind of work was God doing? God began His work in Genesis 2. He wanted to transform Adam who was made of clay into pure gold and precious stone. Thus, the garden of Eden was the beginning of God's work. Ultimately, God will make the garden of Eden into the New Jerusalem. In the garden of Eden God and man had not yet become one, nor had heaven and earth been joined as one. Man did not have the gold within or the precious stone without. From that time on, God began to work in man so that eventually the man of clay would have pure gold inwardly and the precious stone outwardly. On the day that the work of transformation is completely finished, the garden of Eden will have become the New Jerusalem. This is the line of thought from Genesis to Revelation. God's work throughout the generations is to transform the garden of Eden into the New Jerusalem.

In the beginning man was neither pure gold nor precious stone but clay. For this reason, God has been working continuously to reach His goal. At the end of Revelation a city composed of pure gold and precious stones appears. In that city God and man are mingled into one and heaven and earth are joined together. This is the final destination of the saved ones throughout the ages. Hence, we must change our concept. Our concept should not be that one day we will go to a city. Rather, our concept should be to allow God to transform, build, and work Himself into us today so that we may become that city. We are not going to the New Jerusalem but are being built into the New Jerusalem.

The concept of going to heaven is a wrong concept and cannot be found in the Bible. Strictly speaking, our entering into the New Jerusalem is not simply an entering in. It is God's working in us to the point that we have become mature and have been thoroughly dealt with to become pure gold and precious stone. At that time, we will spontaneously be in the

New Jerusalem. Do not think that God will one day put us in the New Jerusalem even if we have not been thoroughly worked on by God and are still men of clay with very little of God's life, the pure gold, inside of us. This is a wrong concept. The correct concept in the Bible is that God is working in us with His life. This requires our cooperation to allow His life to transform us inwardly so that we may be changed from glory to glory (2 Cor. 3:18).

GOD PREPARING THREE PARADISES FOR MAN

If a man dies before he is completely transformed into precious stone, his spirit and soul will go to Hades. The spirits and souls of those who have not been saved go into the fire in Hades, while the spirits and souls of those who have been saved go to the Paradise in Hades and rest there, waiting for God.

Has God's work in the apostle Paul been completed yet? Is Paul's body today made of clay or of precious stone? His body is still made of clay. Our bodies are made of clay, and Paul's body is exactly the same as ours. There is no difference. The only difference is that we are living and he is dead. The nature of Paul's body is the same as the nature of our bodies—it is simply clay. Paul's body is still buried in the earth, but his spirit and soul have gone to a resting place, the Paradise in Hades. God still has unfinished work to do in the believers throughout the ages and generations. Hence, God puts them in Paradise that they may be at rest and may be comforted while waiting for Him to complete His unfinished work in them.

In summary, the Bible clearly states that God has prepared three paradises for man. The first one is the garden of Eden, and the last one is the New Jerusalem. In between these two is the Paradise in Hades. The first paradise was the dwelling place of the man who had just been created by God. This was before the fall of man when there was no sin. The last Paradise is the eternal dwelling place for man after God's work in man has been fully accomplished. In between these two paradises, Satan corrupted man during the process of God's work. As a result, sin and death came in. This problem of death will not be solved until the day of resurrection and transfiguration. At that time death will be swallowed up. However, before that time comes, the problem of death brought in by Satan cannot be solved in man. When it becomes necessary for a man's spirit and soul to leave his body, since God's work in him has not been completed, he cannot enter into the last Paradise, the New Jerusalem. For this reason, God prepared a temporary place for people so that the spirits and souls of those in whom God has not finished His work would have a place to stay. These three places, which the Bible calls paradises, are the places God has prepared and is preparing for all the saved ones.

THREE PARADISES FOR THREE PERIODS OF TIME

God is so gracious to man. Before man's fall, the garden of Eden was the dwelling place for man. It was indeed a paradise, having the tree of life, the river of life, pure gold, and precious stones. The place man will enter into in the future is the New Jerusalem with the new heaven and new earth. This is also a Paradise, even a fuller Paradise. All the saved ones will be in glory there. Today we are somewhere between the beginning and the end. When the spirits and souls of the saved ones leave their bodies, they go to a Paradise of rest and enjoy happiness and comfort there. These three paradises are for the saved ones in three periods of time.

In summary, man lived in the garden of Eden before the fall. This was the first paradise. Then death was brought in after man's fall. Today man has been saved, but death has not yet been swallowed up. Thus, today when believers die, their spirits and souls temporarily go to a place to enjoy rest. This is the Paradise in Hades. When the fullness of time comes and all the work is accomplished, all the saved ones will go to God's eternal dwelling place. This will be the ultimate Paradise. Nevertheless, we must see that this New Jerusalem, the ultimate Paradise, is not for us to walk into or for us to be brought into by God. Rather, God has to work us into it. God will work continuously until the day we are matured and have been completely transformed by Him from glory to glory.

Then we will be exactly the same as Christ, and we will be in the New Jerusalem.

GROWING UNTO MATURITY
TO BECOME THE NEW JERUSALEM

Starting in the garden of Eden, the God of creation began to work in us to make us pure gold and precious stones. When His work is done, we will be in the New Jerusalem. At that time we will not only be in the New Jerusalem, but we will also be able to say that we are the New Jerusalem. It is God who is working heaven into us, and it is God who is working us into the heavenlies (cf. Eph. 2:6). Heaven and man are becoming one. What is heaven? Heaven is the dwelling place of God. When the New Jerusalem is manifested, this dwelling place of God will be us, and we will be the dwelling place. Heaven is being built into us, and we are being built into heaven. We are not only being joined with God but also with heaven. Thus, God's thought is not merely that man would be saved, have his sins forgiven, and have God's life. God wants man to be transformed, to grow in life unto maturity, to let Christ be formed in him, and to be conformed into the Lord's image. Then man will be built up to become the New Jerusalem, the eternal Paradise.

We all need to see this light today. We have been saved, our sins have been forgiven, and we have God's life, but we still must grow in life and become mature. God would never put a man of clay in the New Jerusalem. Every stone built into the New Jerusalem is a precious stone that has been transformed by God. As soon as the life of God gets into man, transformation begins to take place within him to gradually build him into the New Jerusalem. Therefore, strictly speaking, we do not walk into the New Jerusalem. Rather, God works us into it. However, this requires the growth and maturity in life.

To be in the garden of Eden did not require the growth in life. Once man was created, he was put in the garden of Eden. Entering into the Paradise of Hades also does not require the growth in life. Believers simply enter into it when they die. However, to be in the Paradise of the New Jerusalem requires our whole being—our spirit and soul with our body—to be prepared and completely transformed. It requires the growth and maturity in life so that we may participate in God's eternal dwelling place. The cleansing of the precious blood delivers us from sins so that we do not perish. However, whether we can be transformed to become building material for the New Jerusalem depends on the extent to which the life of God grows in us and transforms us. Everyone in the New Jerusalem is a precious stone, not a piece of clay. Thus, the goal of our salvation is not merely to believe but to grow. The goal is not to go to heaven but to grow in life.

Chapter Four

THE NEW JERUSALEM BEING THE ISSUE OF THE UNION OF GOD, HEAVEN, AND MAN

THE NEW JERUSALEM BEING THE HOLY CITY, THE BRIDE, AND THE TABERNACLE OF GOD

Hebrews 11:10 says, "For he eagerly waited for the city which has the foundations, whose Architect and Builder is God." This verse mentions the words *Architect* and *Builder*. Verse 16 says, "They long after a better country, that is, a heavenly one. Therefore God is not ashamed of them, to be called their God." The phrase *to be called their God* means that God belongs to those who are spoken of in this verse. The meaning of this phrase in Greek is very weighty. It means that God is their sole possession. It is not just a title by which God is addressed. Rather, it is a fact indicating that God has become their possession. In other words, God has become the God of those who long after a heavenly country. The end of verse 16 says, "For He has prepared a city for them." This preparation can be done only when there is building. Hebrews 11 says that He has prepared a city, but Revelation 21 says that the city is "prepared as a bride adorned for her husband" (v. 2). The New Jerusalem is a city, yet it is also a bride. Verse 3 continues, "And I heard a loud voice out of the throne, saying, Behold, the tabernacle of God is with men." The New Jerusalem is a city and a bride, but ultimately, it is the tabernacle of God. The tabernacle of God, according to the Old Testament type, is God's habitation.

Then verse 3 continues, saying that God "will tabernacle with them, and they will be His peoples, and God Himself will be with them and be their God." They possess God and own God; thus, God is their God. This very God, whom they possess and own, tabernacles among them. Verse 9 says, "I will show you the bride, the wife of the Lamb," indicating that the bride is the wife of the Lamb, but verse 10 says that this bride is a city, the holy city Jerusalem, which comes down out of heaven from God. Then verse 11 says, "Having the glory of God." This indicates that God tabernacles within His people. Verse 11 also says, "Her light was like a most precious stone, like a jasper stone, as clear as crystal."

The Bible has a continuous line of thought. Revelation 21 repeatedly mentions the matter of stones in describing the New Jerusalem. It says that the light that the city expresses is like a most precious stone (v. 11). It also says that the twelve foundations of the wall of the city are twelve precious stones and that the building work of its wall is jasper, which is also a precious stone (vv. 18-20). First Peter matches this thought. Verse 4 of chapter two says, "Coming to Him, a living stone." The Lord as a living stone is precious to God. Verse 5 says, "You yourselves also, as living stones, are being built up as a spiritual house." When we come to Him, we ourselves also, as living stones, are built up as a spiritual house. The word *built* in this verse is related to the word *Builder* in Hebrews 11:10.

Ephesians 2:20-22 says that we are "being built upon the foundation of the apostles and prophets, Christ Jesus Himself being the cornerstone; in whom all the building, being fitted together, is growing into a holy temple in the Lord; in whom you also are being built together into a dwelling place of God in spirit." These verses also contain the words *stone* and *built.* These verses indicate that the "dwelling place of God in spirit," which is God's habitation, is being produced.

First Corinthians 3:9 says, "You are God's cultivated land, God's building." The cultivated land and the building are connected in this verse. On one hand, the Bible says that we are God's temple, God's building. On the other hand, it says that we are God's harvest, God's land. While the building is something that is built up, the harvest on the land is something that grows up. In this verse the work of God is connected with these two matters of the building and the harvest. In other words, God comes to build the building so that the harvest may grow.

In Matthew 16:18 the Lord said to Peter, "You are Peter, and upon this rock I will build My church." Those who understand Greek know that the name *Peter* means "a little stone." In revealing the church, this verse also mentions the matters of building and stones. Christ is a big stone, the rock upon which the church is built, while Peter is a little stone. Peter, the little stone, had to be built on Christ, the big stone, so that they could become the church, God's habitation. John 14:1-12 is the word that the Lord Jesus spoke to the disciples before He was crucified. The Lord told the disciples that He was going to leave them. The disciples were troubled upon hearing this, but the Lord comforted them by saying, "Do not let your heart be troubled; believe into God, believe also into Me" (v. 1). The Greek phrase translated *believe into God, believe also into Me* also has the meaning "believe into the inside of God, believe into the inside of Me."

The Lord continued, saying, "In My Father's house are many abodes; if it were not so, I would have told you; for I go to prepare a place for you. And if I go and prepare a place for you, I am coming again and will receive you to Myself, so that where I am you also may be" (vv. 2-3). Here the Lord mentions that He is preparing a place, that He is coming again, and that He will bring us to the same place where He is. This is the work that God is doing throughout the generations.

THE GOAL OF THE WORK OF GOD
BEING TO GAIN THE NEW JERUSALEM

The work of God throughout the generations is to gain something that is very mystical. It may be described as a group of people, and it may also be described as an abode, a habitation. It is what Revelation 21 calls the New Jerusalem in the new heaven and new earth. According to what the Bible shows us, the New Jerusalem is the ultimate issue of the work of God in all generations. God began to work in Genesis 1, and by the end of Revelation He has built a holy city, the New Jerusalem. In the beginning of the Bible God shows us the garden of Eden. The garden of Eden is a picture, revealing that God's heart's desire is to produce the New Jerusalem. The New Jerusalem is the ultimate issue of the work of God. This issue is a group of people and also an abode. Revelation clearly says that the New Jerusalem is the bride, the wife of the Lamb (21:9). It also says that the New Jerusalem is the holy city, God's habitation (v. 10).

How can the New Jerusalem be a group of people and a habitation at the same time? How can it simultaneously be a holy city and a bride? Many people cannot understand this. They may ask, "If we are going to be that city in the future, that is, the stones of that city, will we still be able to praise as stones? Will we as stones still have mouths?" These questions prove that our natural mind cannot understand this matter. How can the New Jerusalem be both a city and a woman? It is clearly a group of people, but how can it simultaneously be a place? No matter how long we think about this, we still will not be able to understand. However, although we may not understand or comprehend the revelations of the Bible, we need to believe them.

Revelation 21 tells us that the New Jerusalem is both a city and a bride. This is the clear word in the Bible, and we must believe it no matter what. Actually, the church today is also a mystery. The New Testament clearly states that the church today is constituted with saved people. However, the Bible also says that we are God's temple, God's habitation. We do not need to wait until the time of the new heaven and new earth to be God's habitation, because we are God's habitation today. First Peter 2 says that we are living stones, being built up as a spiritual house by the Lord. A spiritual house is a habitation. Ephesians 2 also says that the apostles and we are being built together on Christ the cornerstone to become God's habitation. Therefore, it is not necessary to wait until the new heaven and new earth for the mystery to be revealed, because it is here today. We who are saved are saints, but we are also a habitation. We are clearly people, but God sees us as living stones. Thus, the New Jerusalem truly has a twofold significance. The work of God in all the ages is to gain the New Jerusalem.

THE NEW JERUSALEM BEING
THE ISSUE OF THE UNION OF GOD, HEAVEN, AND MAN

What is the New Jerusalem? The New Jerusalem is a mingling of God and man, something of God mingled with man. Revelation tells us that the New Jerusalem comes down out of heaven from God. This implies that the New Jerusalem is filled with the element of heaven and is absolutely heavenly. On the other hand, the New Jerusalem is God abiding among man. It is a corporate man. Therefore, the New Jerusalem is something of heaven, God, and also man. This is the revelation in the Bible. According to the verses we have examined, we cannot deny the fact that the ultimate issue of the work of God in every age is to gain something mystical, that is, something of God, man, and heaven mingled together.

There is no question that this holy city, New Jerusalem, comes down out of heaven. When the new heaven and new earth with the New Jerusalem comes down out of heaven to the earth, this union of God, heaven, and man will be on the earth. The ultimate issue of the work of God will be something of God mingled within man and also heaven mingled within man. Heaven, God, and man will be mingled into one as the New Jerusalem. This is the revelation in the Bible. Every saved person will ultimately end up in the heavenly New Jerusalem. This New Jerusalem, according to what Revelation shows us, is God abiding among man and God mingled with man, and it is produced through the transformation of man. When the union of these three is completely manifested, we will be on the new earth. At that time, all of us who are saved will live there with God eternally.

Many Christians are wrongly influenced by Christianity. They think that after a person is saved, he does not need to pay attention to life or to be built up by God but only needs to wait until the day when God will put him into a place called "heaven." However, the Bible shows us that throughout the ages and generations, God has been managing, building, and working on the place into which the believers will ultimately enter. What God has been managing, building, and working on throughout the ages are the saved ones. The principle of God's work on those who have been saved is that He works Himself into them and also works heaven into them. Today we who are saved are not only of God but also of heaven. Not only is God in us, but heaven is also in us.

Ephesians 1 tells us that we are in Christ (v. 12). Then chapter two tells us that we are in the heavenlies (v. 6). We not only have God and Christ in us, but we also have heaven in us. This is not a doctrine but a spiritual fact that can be experienced. Consider your own experience. After you were saved, you may have felt that you had the presence of God and the taste of God within you. At the same time, you also may have felt that heaven was within you. In that experience you may have had a special taste. We not only have the taste of God inside of us but also the taste of heaven. The more we love God and the more we live in God, the more we feel that we are in the heavenlies and inwardly have the taste of heaven, as if heaven has entered into us. This is the experience of every saved one.

Thirty years ago when I was still a young man, no one had ever told me about this; however, whenever I prayed and contacted the Lord, I truly felt as if I were in the heavens, and I was inwardly filled with the taste of heaven. I believe many saints have had this experience. Sometimes when we are about to do something, a sense within will cause us to stop, because we have the feeling inside that we are people in the heavenlies and thus cannot do the earthly things. For example, we may want to buy a piece of fabric, but when we see the color and pattern of the fabric, we may immediately have a feeling inside that as people in the heavenlies we should not wear the colors and patterns that the earthly people wear. Therefore, we may turn around and walk away. Then, while we are walking on the street, we may feel not only the presence of God but also the presence of heaven.

THE WORK OF GOD'S SALVATION BEING
TO WORK GOD AND HEAVEN INTO THE BELIEVERS

I hope that we can see from our experience and the light in the Bible that the work of God's salvation is not only to work God into us but also to work heaven into us. We who are saved are not only a mingling of man with God but also a mingling of man and God with heaven. When we are fellowshipping with the Lord, contacting the Lord, living before the Lord, and walking according to the spirit, do we feel that we are people on the earth or people in heaven? Do we feel that we are inwardly full of heaven or full of the earth? I believe we all have to say that when we are loving the Lord and contacting the Lord, heaven is truly within us, and inwardly we have the taste of heaven and the feeling of heaven.

However, one day we may be tempted, we may fall into the stratagems of Satan, and we may be brought to the slaughter as a lamb. Perhaps one day we go to the movies. At that time we may feel that we, who were in the heavenlies, have fallen into a pit. We may be very uncomfortable inside, the taste of heaven may be gone, and we may have only the taste of earth. Not only going to the movies can make us feel this way, but even the way we adorn and dress ourselves in our daily lives can make us feel this way. When we wear worldly clothes, we often feel like we are dragging a pile of earth onto ourselves and are full of the taste of the earth. This kind of condition is altogether different from the condition we are in when we are contacting the Lord and praying to the Lord. What does this prove? This proves that the work of God in every generation is to work Himself and also heaven into those who have believed into Him. The issue of this work will be the New Jerusalem, which is a union of three entities—God, man, and heaven. This is the place into which we who are saved will ultimately enter.

Again, do not be wrongly influenced by traditional Christianity, thinking that all saved people will "go to heaven." God desires to have the New Jerusalem worked and built into us. We all are parts of the New Jerusalem. You are a part, and I also am a part. All the saved ones throughout the generations are stones in the New Jerusalem.

We who are saved were not originally stones. We were not "Peters" but "Simons." We were originally clay. We were made of clay in order to be burned into bricks. We used to be clay, but because the life of God has entered into us and is changing us inwardly, we are being transformed from clay into stones. What are these stones for? Consider what David did in the Old Testament. After he realized what God's desire was, he wanted to build a holy temple for God. He first sent people to hew stones out of the mountains. Then they shaped each stone into a certain size and polished the stones until they were shiny. One day King Solomon came and transported these stones to Jerusalem, and by arranging them and laying them one by one, he built the holy temple. The Bible says that while Solomon was building the temple, neither the sound of a hammer nor of an ax nor of any iron tool was heard (1 Kings 6:7). Those sounds had been heard in the mountains when the people had been hewing out the stones during the time of King David. King Solomon then took the stones that David had prepared and arranged and laid them to build up the holy temple.

THE LORD BEING TODAY'S DAVID
PREPARING MATERIAL FOR GOD

Our Lord is today's David. He is preparing us, stones who have been taken from the mountains of this world. Today the sounds of hammers, axes, and other iron tools striking stone can be heard among us. Perhaps our husbands or wives are our hammers, those coordinating with us in the church are our axes, and our children are the other iron tools. The difficulties in all of our environments strike us to deal with us and to prepare us as stones. Never treat the matter of building in the Bible as something simple. We all know that stones cannot be piled up randomly to construct a building. To be built, stones first need to be dealt with—all the protruding corners and sharp edges must be removed, and the places that are not smooth enough must be ground smooth. This is the building work that God is doing on us. Do not view the matter of building only as something that is very sweet and simple. When God comes to work on us, I fear that very few among us are able to bear it.

Today it seems as if everyone among us is on the same plane. When we do things, we are very polite, nobody touches anyone in the wrong way, and we get along with one another peacefully. Therefore, there is no building or construction. The stones are here, but they are all lying flat in the same plane or dimension. There is no three-dimensional building. If you and I were willing to give ourselves to God and let Him do the work of building, I am afraid that we would all have many corners and sharp edges that would need to be hacked off, pounded with hammers, and beaten with iron tools. God has to work on us so that we can be built together.

THE NEW JERUSALEM BEING
THE FULL CONSUMMATION OF THE CHURCH

Some people say that the Lord is building the church, not the New Jerusalem. This kind of thought is foolish. Ephesians 2, 1 Peter 2, and Matthew 16 show us that today God is saving us and working on us to build us into God's habitation. Today we are the habitation that God is building. One day the new heaven and new earth will appear in which will be the habitation, the New Jerusalem. Therefore, the habitation that God is building today is the church, and the habitation in the future will be the New Jerusalem. These are not two habitations but one habitation. If they were two habitations, I am afraid that in the future we would be abandoned. If they were two habitations, then today in the age of grace God would build us into the church, His habitation, and then in the future God would abandon us and build the New Jerusalem, a larger habitation. God is not like this. The church as His habitation today is a precursor of the New Jerusalem as His habitation in the future. The church is a miniature of the ultimate habitation. The New Jerusalem as God's habitation is the full consummation of the church as His habitation.

Throughout the generations, God has not been building two habitations in the universe—one on the earth as the church and one in the heavens as the New Jerusalem. In all the generations, God has not had two works but one work. The Lord Jesus said that He was going to prepare a place for us, and He also said that He would build the church upon Himself as the rock. These two statements do not mean that the Lord had two works—one work of building the church on the earth and one work of preparing the New Jerusalem in heaven. Rather, the Lord has only one work—the church that

He is building on the earth is the New Jerusalem that He is preparing in the heavens.

Hebrews 11 says that God is building a city. That building is the spiritual house mentioned in 1 Peter 2 and also God's habitation mentioned in Ephesians 2. Today the building is being built on a small scale. Today it is merely a house, a spiritual house, but when it reaches full completion in the future, it will be a city, something much larger in scale. Therefore, we can see that God has only one work in the universe today, that is, to build an abode for Himself. The miniature of this abode is the church today, the spiritual house which is His habitation. Ultimately, at the time of completion, it will be a holy city and a tabernacle, the mutual abode of God and man. Please remember that the church and the New Jerusalem are not two parallel entities. Rather, the church and the New Jerusalem are connected to one another. The church is a precursor of the New Jerusalem, and the New Jerusalem is the consummation of the church. The two are one. God's building of the church is also His building of the New Jerusalem. God's building in us is the building of the church and also the building of the eternal abode in the future. This is a very mysterious concept. One day we will all realize that the habitation or abode that God is building in every age is a union of three entities—Him, us, and heaven. The New Jerusalem in the future will be our eternal abode, a city built by God through all the generations.

THE UNION OF THE THREE— GOD, MAN, AND HEAVEN— BEING THE BUILDING MATERIAL OF GOD

What kind of material is God using to build His habitation? God is mingling Himself into our being and also adding heaven into us. Thus, the material is the union of three entities—God, man, and heaven. This is like the materials that a cement worker uses to make concrete, which is a mixture of sand, crushed stones, and cement. The three—God, man, and heaven—are being mingled and built together, and one day, when they are ready and manifested, they will be the New Jerusalem. Therefore, the eternal abode that we will ultimately enter into is not something unrelated to us today or something completely objective to us.

We who are stones are the materials of the city that God has been building throughout the ages. God will keep working on us and building us, the stones, until a city is built at the end. God, man, and also heaven will be in that city. Heaven will be in it, God will be in it, and man will also be in it. However, the heaven in the New Jerusalem will not merely be heaven; it will be heaven mingled within man. God will be there, as well as His glory, life, nature, and image. However, in the New Jerusalem God will not be purely God but God mingled within man. Man will also be there. The twelve foundations of the wall of the city have the twelve names of the twelve apostles. The stone that has Peter's name signifies the man Peter. Therefore, man will truly be there. Not only the ones in the New Testament will be there, but the names of the twelve tribes of the sons of Israel in the Old Testament are also there, indicating that they will be there as well.

THE WAY OF BUILDING THE NEW JERUSALEM BEING THE WAY OF LIFE

Therefore, the New Jerusalem is not merely man. Rather, it is man mingled with God. Furthermore, it is not only man mingled with God but also God and man mingled with heaven, the three mingled into one. This is truly a mystery, showing us that the way of the eternal abode is the way of life. Do not think that even if we do not grow today or as men of clay we are not transformed and remain what we are, then one day we will simply enter into the New Jerusalem. Can a man of clay who has not been transformed be put among precious stones? Is he worthy of such a thing? Of course he is not. This is not the case. It is by our growth in life and by our being transformed continually unto maturity that we will one day become fully mature, issuing in the New Jerusalem. It is not a matter of entering in or going up but of allowing God to build us and work us into the New Jerusalem. This is the way of the New Jerusalem, the way of life.

Do you want to be a part of that eternal abode? If so, you

must let God work in you to such an extent that you become a part of that eternal abode. Some saints have said that they truly want to mature but that they do not know the way to reach maturity. In the past they thought that everything would be all right if they only believed in the precious blood of Jesus. They did not care about their condition or whether they overcame or failed. They thought that as long as they were saved and were justified in His blood, they would definitely "go to heaven." However, now they are worried, because they realize that to be a part of God's eternal abode requires maturity in life. How can we mature? What is the way to become mature? The answer can be found in 1 Corinthians 3:9, which tells us that we are God's cultivated land, God's building. God's building is His cultivating. This means that the way to grow unto maturity is to let God build within us and to allow God to work within us. This is not a heavy doctrine but a very personal experience. We have to allow the Spirit to work within us, to touch our difficulties, to hew our corners and sharp edges, and to move and operate within us. If we do not allow Him to work within us and do not let Him build within us, we cannot have the growth and maturity in life. His building is our growth; His work is our maturity.

We have to pay the price to answer His demand within us. What is the way to maturity? The way is to let God work in us. He is a living God. He is in us ruling, restricting, touching, motivating, and turning us. In order to be willing to let Him be everything to us, to work in us, and to build in us, we have to pay the price. How do we pay the price? We pay the price by following His feelings within us. We need to follow whatever we sense in our spirit, the deepest part within us. If we let God work and build in us, then we will be blessed. We will be the stones prepared and ready in God's hands. When the Lord comes, our life will be manifested. He will have built us together one by one. One stone will be Peter, another will be Paul, and another may be you or me. Thus, the city, the New Jerusalem, is being built piece by piece. Therefore, the eternal abode is not something we enter into but something we grow into. If we let God work within us, then we will grow, become mature, and ultimately grow to be the New Jerusalem.

CHAPTER FIVE

THE WAY GOD BUILDS HIMSELF INTO MAN

Ephesians 4:12-13 says, "For the perfecting of the saints unto the work of the ministry, unto the building up of the Body of Christ, until we all arrive at the oneness of the faith and of the full knowledge of the Son of God, at a full-grown man, at the measure of the stature of the fullness of Christ." These two verses put two matters together. Verse 12 speaks of the building up of the Body of Christ, and verse 13 speaks of the growth of the Body unto a full-grown man, unto the measure of the stature of the fullness of Christ. The building up in verse 12 refers to the growth in verse 13. Revelation 19:7 says, "For the marriage of the Lamb has come, and His wife has made herself ready." We need to pay attention to the phrase *His wife has made herself ready*. Matthew 25:1-13 speaks of the parable of the ten virgins. This shows us that God's work throughout the generations is to build Himself into man. He is the God of heaven, possessing not only the nature of God but also the element of heaven. When He builds Himself into us, He constitutes the nature of God and the element of heaven into us. The more we allow Him to work Himself into us, the more we will have the element of God and the element of heaven. We all have had this experience. When we submit to the Holy Spirit, allowing God to work Himself into us, we have the presence of God and the taste of heaven within us.

THE CHURCH AS THE MINGLING
OF GOD, HEAVEN, AND MAN
BEING A MINIATURE OF THE NEW JERUSALEM

God, heaven, and man are mingled as one, and the mingling

of the three is the church today. What is the church? The church is God and heaven mingled together with man. This surely is a mystery. Those who have not received God's salvation cannot comprehend this matter. The unbelievers are merely human, but we who are saved have the all-inclusive Christ living in us. We are something mystical because we have God and heaven inside of us. This is the church today.

The church is a miniature, similar to a fetus in a mother's womb, which is conceived as a miniature of a complete person. Gradually, the fetus grows and eventually is born as a complete person. The church, which is something mystical, is a miniature, and when it is completed, it will be the New Jerusalem.

THE WAY FOR THE SAINTS TO GROW IN LIFE

A newborn child actually begins as a fetus in the mother's womb, and this fetus grows bit by bit until it is born. The church today is a miniature of the glorious New Jerusalem in the future, and it will continually grow until the day that it is fully grown. How can the church or the saved ones grow continuously? We grow through God's continuous building work in us. The more God builds, the more we grow. Without God's building work we cannot grow. Do not think that you can grow by yourself. Our growing is actually God's building. Ephesians 4:12-13 clearly shows us that the building is the growing.

We cannot grow if we do not have God within us building Himself into us. We should all spend time to find out how God builds and how we can grow. God's building and our growth are for the preparation of the bride. Revelation 19:7 says that the bride has made herself ready. What does it mean to say that the bride has made herself ready? It means that the church has been built up. The bride signifies the church in its ultimate state. The bride having made herself ready means that the church has been completely built up and has grown unto maturity. Therefore, if we find out how God builds, we will see how we can grow and make ourselves ready.

THE WAY TO BE READY

The parable of the virgins in Matthew 25 shows us the

way to get ready. Simply speaking, this parable reveals that when the Lord comes back, those who are ready will sit with Him at the wedding feast. To be ready here means that the bride has made herself ready, that God has completed His building work in man, and that we have grown and matured in the Lord's life. These three matters—God's building in us, our growth in the Lord's life, and our getting ready before the Lord—are all linked together. God's building work in us is our growth in the Lord's life and is also our getting ready before the Lord. These three matters—God's building, our growth, and our getting ready—are actually one matter. How does the Lord carry out the building work in us? When we were saved, He not only forgave our sins, but through His Spirit He entered into us with His life to be our life. That was the beginning of His building work.

An unsaved person is merely a human being. But we who are genuinely saved have God's Holy Spirit and God's life within us. We are not merely humans but humans with the life of God and the Holy Spirit mingled within. When the Holy Spirit of God and the life of God entered into us, that was the beginning of God's building work in us.

THE WAY GOD BUILDS HIMSELF INTO MAN BEING FIRSTLY THE BREAKING OF THE SELF

From the time that God begins His building work in us onward, the Spirit of God continuously moves us and motivates us within, and the life of God continuously operates and works within us. Both the moving of the Spirit of God and the operating of the life of God are God's building work within us. This kind of building work requires our cooperation, mainly in the matter of the breaking of our self. If the self is not broken, it is impossible for God to build Himself into us. How much God can build Himself into us depends on how much we allow God to break us. Those who do not allow God to break them cannot have God Himself built into them.

It may be difficult for some to understand how God breaks us or how God builds Himself into us. To illustrate, when we are sick, the doctor often must give us an injection and a prescription. Because we may lack the proper nutrients or vitamins, the doctor must inject the nutrients or vitamins into us. What is his first step in doing this? He must first "'break" our body. He must insert a needle into our flesh in order to inject the nutrients into our body. If there is no opening in our body, the nutrients cannot be injected into us. Likewise, if we do not allow God to break us or to make an opening in us, then God Himself cannot enter into us. Perhaps some people may say that they understand this. However, what is it that God wants to break in us? The injection given by the doctor breaks our physical flesh. Similarly, in order for God to build Himself into us and to enter into us, He needs to break our "flesh"—our soul-life, our self. God has to break our self so that He can enter into us and build Himself into us.

What is the soul-life or the self? Practically, the self refers to our thoughts, preferences, and opinions. All the activities in our mind are actions of the soul, our self. Our thoughts, views, preferences, choices, opinions, and decisions all represent our self and are all part of our self. When God comes to break our self, He comes to break all these things. What has to be broken? Our views, thoughts, preferences, choices, opinions, and decisions all need to be broken. If we allow God to break all these things, then God will have an opening in us, and then He will be able to inject Himself into us.

THE REASON GOD IS UNABLE
TO BUILD HIMSELF INTO SOME BELIEVERS

Some people may say that they understand this doctrine well but that it is still very troublesome to them and unclear in their practice. For example, you may be a genuinely saved person with the Spirit of God and the life of God in you. However, your views, insight, thoughts, opinions, preferences, choices, ideas, and decisions may be intact and altogether yours. Thus, not one bit of God's element can be injected into you. Though you are saved and the Spirit of God and the life of God are in you, your thoughts and views do not have the element of God in them. God has no access to your thoughts and views and has no ground in your preferences and choices. In your ideas and decisions you keep God outside the door.

Although we have the life of God and the Spirit of God in us, we may handle things as if we do not have God in us. Though we have God's life and God's Spirit dwelling within us, God may not have the ground in us when we make choices or decisions.

In other words, although all those who are saved have the Spirit of God and the life of God within them, God may not have the ground in their thoughts, preferences, and views, that is, in their soul. This is the main reason why there is no growth in life in many saved ones and why God cannot build Himself into them.

THE SPIRIT MOVING MAN
TO RECEIVE GOD'S BREAKING

How does God build Himself into each part of our being? God first needs to break our thoughts, ideas, preferences, views, choices, and opinions. How much God can build Himself into us depends on how much God has broken us. For example, suppose a brother would like to arrange his children's marriages. The brother is indeed a saved person, having God's Spirit and God's life within. But when he is dealing with his children regarding the matter of marriage, he does not give any ground to God in his thoughts and views. When he worships God, God has the ground, but when he considers his children's marriages, he puts God aside. In the matter of his children's marriages, his thoughts and insight do not have God's element. Therefore, in this matter he does not have God.

This brother may have very little of God's element in him, so God's desire is to build more of His element into him. In the brother's insight, thinking, and determination, he still may lack the element of God. Therefore, God has no ground in his view of his children's marriages. What can God do in such a situation? If God has mercy on him and is gracious to him, He will continue His building work within him. How will God do this building work in him? He will do it by breaking his insight and thinking. First, God must move him through the Spirit like a doctor giving an injection. While he is being punctured, he may have a sense of pain, which may remind him that his thinking and determination for his children's marriages have all been from himself and without God. The Spirit then may move and pierce him a little more so that he will feel sorry, mournful, and regretful. During this time, if he humbles himself and receives the piercing and moving of the Spirit, God's element will be built up in him more and more.

On the day of Pentecost, the Spirit moved in men, and many of them felt their hearts being pricked (Acts 2:37). When a doctor gives injections to people, they feel the pricking of the needle. The work of the Spirit inside us is very often like the piercing of a needle. His particular moving pierces our thoughts and preferences. One day the Spirit will pierce our view concerning our children's marriages and our plans for our career and our future. He will be like a doctor giving an injection, piercing our skin and flesh, so that we will have a sense of pain and feel mournful. If we are willing to humble ourselves and receive the moving of the Spirit, then the Spirit will inject God's intention into our thinking, determination, and preferences. Then our thoughts and views toward our children's marriages will give more ground to God and have more of God's element. Thus, God will do a further building work in us. With the increase of God's element within us, God's life will then expand and grow.

GOD'S DEALING

However, sometimes when the Spirit moves and pierces the heart of a brother, he is unwilling to comply. He still behaves and thinks according to his own insight and views and handles his children's marriages according to his own thinking. One day, if God has mercy on him and is gracious to him, God will stretch out His hand and raise up an environment to smite him. This smiting is God's dealing in order to deal with his insight and views, which are devoid of God. This brother may encounter trouble at work, his health may begin to deteriorate, or his daughter-in-law may cause trouble in the family. At this moment, this brother, having been inwardly pierced by God, may awaken and realize that in the matter of his children's marriages he did not give any ground to God or let God in and that he acted altogether according to his own insights, views, preferences, and opinions. This painful realization will be God's dealing in order to break his thinking, opinions, preferences, and ideas.

Once this brother is broken, God will be able to come in and gain ground. This person's insight and thinking will then have God's element. God will expand outward in him and will go a step further in the work of building. Simultaneously, he will grow more, become more mature, and become more ready. If all the saints continually allow God to build in them, grow in them, and prepare them in this way, then they would be on the way to arrive at full maturity and to become the New Jerusalem.

PAYING THE PRICE TO BUY THE OIL

Matthew 25:4 shows us that the wise virgins not only carried their lamps but also prepared their vessels with oil. They were those who paid the price to buy oil and to make themselves ready. What is the meaning of paying the price to buy oil and to make ourselves ready? In the Bible oil signifies the Spirit who is God Himself. To buy oil is to pay the price to gain God. No matter what we wish to gain, we must pay a price in order to gain it. In order to make ourselves ready, we have to gain more of the Spirit and more of God. To gain more of God and more of the Spirit requires that we pay a price. For example, the brother in our previous example needed to pay the price of letting go of his insight and views in the matter of his children's marriages. To put it more directly, his insight and views had to be broken so that God could come into his insight and views. This is to pay the price and to buy the oil. If we pay the price and let God have the ground and the freedom in us in every single matter, then we will be filled with God and possessed by God. Inwardly, we will be full of oil, full of the Holy Spirit, that is, full of God Himself. When we are filled to the uttermost, then we will be matured, and God's building will be completed.

CHAPTER SIX

THE WAY FOR A CHRISTIAN TO MATURE IN LIFE— WATCHING AND BEING READY

In Matthew 24:40-44 the Lord gave us two commands. The first command is found in verse 42, which says, "Watch therefore." The second command is found in verse 44, which says, "You also be ready." We need to watch and be ready. When we come to 25:1-13, the Lord commands us once again, saying, "Watch therefore" (v. 13). This command is the same as that in 24:42. At the same time, 25:10 also mentions the matter of being ready, telling us that those who are ready can enter into the feast with the Lord. We can see that both Matthew 24 and 25 tell us to watch and be ready.

WATCHING AND BEING READY BEING THE WAY FOR A CHRISTIAN TO MATURE IN LIFE

The matter of watching and being ready is related to a Christian's maturity. Although the above passages do not mention the word *maturity,* they repeatedly mention the words *watch* and *be ready.* A person who is ready must certainly be mature. To watch and be ready is the way to become mature. No other passages in the Bible show us more clearly the way for a Christian to become mature than Matthew 24 and 25. The way to become mature is to watch and be ready. Those who are ready are the mature ones.

It is easy for Christians to tend to emphasize the teachings in the Gospel of John but to neglect those in the Gospels of Matthew and Mark. For instance, when we preach the gospel, we often like to use John 3:16, which says, "For God so loved the world that He gave His only begotten Son, that every one who believes into Him would not perish, but would have eternal life." We also often use 15:5, which says, "I am the vine; you are the branches. He who abides in Me and I in him...." We often speak about these verses in the church meetings, but few of us pay attention to the teachings in the Gospels of Matthew and Mark. The Bible not only contains the Gospel of John, which tells us that those who believe into the Son will have eternal life, but also the Gospels of Matthew and Mark, which tell us that there is a kingdom into which we should seek to enter. We gain eternal life once we believe into the Lord. However, we need to follow the Lord for a while before we can gain the heavenly kingdom.

John tells us how to abide in the Lord after we have received the Lord's life. Matthew speaks of how to follow the Lord after we have become His disciples. John 15 is the Lord's teaching before He was crucified. Matthew 24 and 25 are prophecies that were also spoken by the Lord before He was crucified. We should pay as much attention to the Gospel of Matthew as we do to the Gospel of John. It is a pity that today in the church we often emphasize the teachings in John but neglect those in Matthew. We believe that in these last days the Lord will gradually recover the teachings in Matthew. John only tells us how the life that is in us grows, but Matthew shows us how this life matures and how we can be made ready for the Lord's coming. In other words, Matthew tells us what kind of condition we need to be in before we can meet the Lord. If we truly hope to be with the Lord and to abide with Him, we must know the condition we must be in and the stage that we must reach.

THOSE WHO ARE READY BEING TAKEN, AND THOSE WHO ARE NOT READY BEING LEFT BEHIND

Let us consider Matthew 24 and 25. First, we need to see the similarities between these two portions of the Bible. They are similar in their topics. Both portions contain similar points about the Lord and about us. Regarding the Lord, both chapters say that the Lord will come. Regarding us, both chapters say that we need to watch and be ready. Thus, the subject of these two portions is that we need to watch and be ready and that we need to wait for the Lord's coming and bring Him back. These are two different passages, but they have one topic.

It can be said that the first portion, Matthew 24, is an explicit message to those who belong to the Lord, telling them how to watch and be ready while waiting to meet the Lord. We all know that the Lord will come. Therefore, we should watch and be ready. If we are ready, we will be taken. If we are not ready, we will be left behind. Thus, verse 40 says, "At that time two men will be in the field; one is taken and one is left." The one who is taken is ready to be taken to see the Lord. Undoubtedly, the one who is left is not ready yet. This does not happen because the one who is taken is saved and the one who is left is not saved. Both men are in the field. They both have the same life, are on the same ground, and do the same thing. Hence, there is no doubt that both of them are saved. Although both of them are saved, having the same status, position, and kind of living, and although they are doing the same thing, yet they are different in the matter of their maturity in life. One is ready in life and thus is raptured, while the other is not ready and is left behind.

Verse 41 goes on to say, "Two women will be grinding at the mill; one is taken and one is left." Like the two men, the two women have the same status, position, job, and kind of living. Both are saved. It is not that one is grinding while the other is watching a movie, so the one who is grinding is taken while the one who is watching a movie is left. Both women are the same in status, ground, living, job, and career. If they are the same, then why is one taken and the other left? Verses 42 to 44 tell us that the reason is related to the need to watch and be ready. One is taken because she is watchful and ready. The other is left because she is not watchful and ready. Although their status, position, career, and living are the same and both are saved, they differ in one aspect. They differ in their attitude toward the Lord's coming. One is watchful and ready, but the other is neither watchful nor ready.

We have all been saved and may be meeting together and living the Christian life together. Outwardly, there may be no difference between one saint and another. However, our attitudes toward the Lord and His coming may vary. Some saints may be watchful and ready, waiting for the Lord's coming. Some may be indifferent to the Lord's coming. They may merely want to be common. They may not want to be watchful or ready in regard to the Lord and His coming. Thus, when the Lord comes to take His people, those who are ready will be taken. Those who are not, although they are saved, will be left for some time. The Lord's message in Matthew 24 shows us this difference.

Do not think that as long as you are saved, are meeting together with other Christians, and are apparently the same as they are, you will have no problems. The Lord's thought toward us in Matthew 24 is, "You have to be watchful and ready, because to be saved is one thing and to wait for My coming is another. To be a believer is one thing and to be watchful and ready is another." For instance, suppose a person has eight children. To beget them is one matter, but to raise them up and educate them is another. All eight of them belong to the same parents, are in the same family, have the same life, and live the same kind of lives. Outwardly, it may seem that there are no differences among them, but actually there are. How will each one grow up? How will they receive their education? How will they prepare themselves to be useful people? In these aspects there are often differences.

The children may all have the same parents. They may belong to the same family and may have the same kind of lives. However, how they are educated, how they prepare themselves, how they live their lives, and which ways they take all depend on how they grow up and prepare themselves from childhood to adulthood.

In view of this example, the attitude that we have toward the Lord and His coming—whether watchful and ready or indifferent—is very important because it will determine whether we will be taken or left behind. Therefore, the Lord commanded us again and again to watch and be ready. We not only must accept the word in John that we will have eternal life if we believe in the Lord, but we must also accept the Lord's command in Matthew 24 to watch and be ready. This was not only the Lord's word but also His teaching before leaving the world. On the Mount of Olives before He departed, He told the disciples to watch and be ready. Why? He told them this because if they were not watchful or ready, there was a chance that they might be left behind. Like the two men in the field, one would be taken and one would be left. Therefore, in order not to be left, we must be watchful and ready.

THE PARABLE OF THE VIRGINS

By now we all realize that it is not sufficient to merely be a Christian. We must also be watchful, ready, and mature in life in order to go before the Lord. However, what is the way to become watchful and ready, and how can we be matured in life? In all matters the truth must first be presented and then the way. Matthew 24 states the truth—one needs to be watchful and ready in order to be taken and not left behind. The way is in Matthew 25. In Matthew 25 the Lord used a parable to illustrate the way to become watchful and ready. The portion in chapter twenty-four states the truth, and the portion in chapter twenty-five shows the way. The Lord first gave us a clear message on the truth of being watchful and ready and then pointed out to us the way to be watchful and ready. A truth without a way is useless. We may say that we need to be watchful and ready, but if we do not know how to be watchful and do not understand how to get ready, the truth does not help us much.

The Lord showed us the way to be watchful and ready in Matthew 25. What is the way? The Lord used an illustration. We often need to use illustrations when providing people directions, such as a drawing a map to show the way. In Matthew 25 the Lord used the parable of the virgins to show us the way to be watchful and ready. While chapter twenty-four states the truth, chapter twenty-five shows us the way. While chapter twenty-four speaks about two women grinding, chapter twenty-five speaks about ten virgins preparing oil. This is very meaningful. Two plus ten equals twelve. In the Bible the church in its ultimate stage is represented by the number twelve. The New Jerusalem has twelve gates and twelve foundations, and on them are the names of the twelve apostles in the New Testament and the twelve tribes in the Old Testament. The tree of life produces twelve fruits, and the wall of the city is 144 cubits high, which is the product of twelve times twelve. Thus, ultimately, the church will be represented by the number twelve. The number twelve signifies eternal completion.

Why then in Matthew 24 through 25 did the Lord separate twelve people into groups of two and ten as if He were dividing the church into two groups? The two in Matthew 24 were either working in the field or grinding at home. They were both working and were involved in some form of activity. Undoubtedly, they signify the living believers. When the Lord comes, only a minority of the believers will be alive. The majority will be dead and asleep. The ten virgins in Matthew 25 were all sleeping. They were not sleeping spiritually or sleeping because they were not being watchful. Rather, their bodies were physically sleeping. The five foolish ones were sleeping, as were the five prudent ones. This shows us that they were not sleeping spiritually or sleeping because they were not being watchful. Instead, their bodies were physically sleeping. Why were they sleeping? They were sleeping because the bridegroom had delayed. Because the Lord has delayed, even Paul, who was the most watchful one, became drowsy and fell asleep. To become drowsy is to get old and to become sick, and to sleep is to pass away. These ten virgins signify the majority of the believers who will have died by the time the Lord comes. When the Lord comes, most of the saved ones in the past ages will have already fallen asleep. Paul and Peter who were watchful and who loved the Lord are asleep. Demas who loved the world but not the Lord is also asleep. They are all asleep. Why is this? They are asleep because the Lord has delayed. When the bridegroom delayed, the two groups of virgins became drowsy and fell asleep. This means that they all got old, became sick, and finally passed away. They signify the majority of the believers.

When the Lord comes, only a minority of the believers will still be living. If we read the Bible carefully, we will find that the Bible often separates a group of twelve into groups of ten and two. For example, out of the twelve tribes in the Old

Testament, ten tribes rebelled and became the kingdom of Israel, while the other two tribes remained as the kingdom of Judah. Another example is the twelve apostles. In one case, while two of the apostles fought to sit on the Lord's right hand and left hand, the other ten were unhappy with them. The Bible often divides the number twelve into ten and two. The number ten signifies the majority, and the number two signifies the remnant. When the Lord comes, most of the believers throughout the ages will have fallen asleep. Only a minority will still be living. Thus, the truth in Matthew 24 refers to the living believers, whereas the way in Matthew 25 refers to the believers who have died. However, whether a believer is alive or dead, he needs to be watchful and ready, and the way to be watchful and ready is the same for both the living and the dead.

The Status and Position of a Virgin

First, at the beginning of Matthew 25 the Lord said, "At that time the kingdom of the heavens will be likened to ten virgins, who took their lamps and went forth to meet the bridegroom" (v. 1). This shows us that the status and position of those who belong to the Lord is that of a virgin. The word for *virgin* used by the Jews has the same meaning as the word used by the Chinese. In China a virgin never leaves her house. She is always hidden and shut inside her chamber. The status and position of a Christian on this earth should be like that of a virgin. He should be hidden, having little involvement or contact with the outside world, and he should be pure and sanctified.

The Condition of a Virgin

Second, all the virgins took their lamps. This indicates that they were in the night. At nighttime it is dark, and lamps are needed. Today's age is the age of darkness. In this world of darkness Christians should shine like lamps. What the Lord meant in Matthew 25 was that those who belong to the Lord have lamps in their hands. They have light and can shine in the dark. A person who truly belongs to the Lord is always much brighter than the unbelievers. However, it is a pity that many saints have forsaken their status as virgins and do not take their lamps and shine as they should.

The Way of a Virgin

Third, the way of the virgins is that they went forth; that is, they went out from their original place. This is what it means to be a Christian. We were born into the world and were raised up in the world. The world was where we lived. However, after we were saved, we became people who are going out of this world.

The Life of a Virgin

Fourth, why did the virgins go out? They went out because they wanted to meet the bridegroom. This tells us that there should be only one purpose in our life and work—to meet the Lord and to wait for His coming.

I hope that the Holy Spirit would speak to us and reveal to us that a Christian's status and position is that of a virgin, his condition is to take his lamp to shine, his way is to go out of the world, and the purpose of his life is to wait for the Lord's coming. Only such a Christian is a normal Christian. May we all have ears to hear. If we do not heed these words, then these words will not save us but condemn us when we meet the Lord.

Please do not forget that on June 12, 1955 a man in Manila cried out to you, saying, "The Lord is commanding us to watch and be ready and to be virgins taking our lamps and going forth to meet the Bridegroom." You cannot say that you have not heard these words. These words are the gospel and words of salvation. If you do not receive them, they will condemn you one day. I hope we would not be indifferent. May we all receive these words and repent of our past condition. May we be virgins, taking our shining lamps and going out of this world to meet Christ our Bridegroom.

CHAPTER SEVEN

THE WAY FOR A CHRISTIAN
TO MATURE IN LIFE—
THE FILLING OF THE HOLY SPIRIT

In Revelation 3:15 and 18 the Lord said to the church in Laodicea, "I know your works, that you are neither cold nor hot; I wish that you were cold or hot....I counsel you to buy from Me gold refined by fire that you may be rich, and white garments that you may be clothed and that the shame of your nakedness may not be manifested, and eyesalve to anoint your eyes that you may see." Here the Lord mentions the phrase *to buy*. We all know that to buy something means to pay a price for it.

THE STATUS, CONDITION, WAY, AND LIVING
OF A CHRISTIAN

In the parable of the virgins in Matthew 25 we clearly see that we who are Christians should have the status of a pure and simple virgin. In our condition we should be holding forth our lamps, which shine in and illuminate the darkness. The way that we take should lead us out of the world, which does not want the Lord. And the purpose of our living should be to await and meet the Lord. Since our Lord is not in the world and the world does not want Him, we should not have a lingering love for the world. Our hearts should not be occupied with this world. We have to leave this world. We must come out of the world in order to receive our Lord, the unique Bridegroom.

What grieves our hearts today is that many Christians do not know what their status and condition should be. If we would consider our condition, we would realize that we not only are not up to where we should be but are far from it. We are not like virgins. In our condition we are not holding our lamps and shining forth. Neither are we leaving the world, which does not want the Lord, nor are we receiving and waiting for the Lord. In the Gospel of Matthew the Lord pointed out four aspects of the proper situation of a Christian—his status, condition, way, and living. However, these aspects are merely the beginning or starting point for the kind of living that a Christian must have.

THE STARTING POINT OF THE CHRISTIAN LIFE

If we do not have these four aspects, we should bow our heads, saying, "Lord, forgive me. I have not begun my Christian life. Although I have become a Christian, have the name of a Christian, and have been baptized to enter into the church, I am not like a virgin. I do not have the light of a lamp shining in me. My steps have not led me out of this world, and I have not been waiting for You and preparing myself to meet You." Many of us must admit that we have not begun our Christian life. We are Christians in name but not in reality. We do not stand in our position as Christians. We do not have the proper condition of a Christian. We do not walk the way of a Christian, nor do we live the life of a Christian. However, even if we do have these four aspects, we should not assume that we are qualified and mature enough to see the Lord. Please remember that these aspects are only the starting point, not the end. We have only started to grow and have not yet reached maturity.

THE PROGRESS OF THE CHRISTIAN LIFE— BEING A PRUDENT VIRGIN

The Lord Reminding and Warning the Foolish

Every saved person should have these four aspects and should continue to grow in them. In the parable of the virgins the Lord deliberately said, "And five of them were foolish and five were prudent. For the foolish, when they took their lamps, did not take oil with them; but the prudent took oil in their vessels with their lamps" (Matt. 25:2-4). The Lord pointed

out that these ten virgins were different and that the difference was not whether they were genuine or false but whether
they were prudent or foolish. The Lord divided them into two
groups—five were foolish and five were prudent. It was not
that one group was genuinely saved while the other group
was falsely saved, as some Bible expositors say. The ten virgins
were all genuinely saved. The Lord pointed out that what He
was concerned about was not the matter of genuineness versus
falseness but prudence versus foolishness. His concern was
whether they were foolish or prudent.

Whether the virgins were genuine or false is a matter
related to their nature. Whether they were foolish or prudent
is a matter related to their condition. In their nature they were
genuine and proper because they were all virgins and were
all saved. However, in their conditions they were different, not
the same. One group was foolish and the other group was prudent. All saved ones are not necessarily the same. There may
be a difference. You may be a saved person belonging to
the Lord, but you may be either prudent or foolish. Therefore,
we all have to see that it is not enough to be saved. We also
have to consider whether we are foolish or prudent. This
means that a person who is saved, a Christian, has to take a
further step to determine what kind of Christian he will be.
Will he be foolish or prudent? Here the Lord first mentioned
the foolish, showing that He was primarily warning the foolish ones. Of course the prudent ones do not need this
teaching. Only those who are foolish need this teaching. The
Lord reminded the foolish ones so that they would be watchful and prepared.

Five Being the Number of Responsibility

In the Bible the number twelve indicates eternal perfection, whereas the number ten indicates human perfection.
Everyone has ten fingers and ten toes. The Chinese speak
of perfection, but the perfection that they refer to is human
perfection. The Lord divided the ten virgins into two groups of
five. The number five in the Bible is the number of responsibility. For example, each of our hands has five fingers. Our
fingers do not consist of three fingers plus two fingers but

four fingers plus one thumb. This is very meaningful. If we took away our thumb, it would be difficult for us to do things with only our four fingers. Whatever we do requires that we use our thumb along with our other four fingers. The four fingers plus the one thumb enables us to work. Hence, we can bear responsibility.

Some may ask what the addition of four plus one means. In the Bible the number four is the number related to created beings. There are four living creatures in the book of Revelation. These four living creatures signify the created beings. The number one signifies the unique God as the Creator. The addition of four plus one signifies the created beings plus God the Creator. Those who have not believed into the Lord and are not saved are merely creatures, created people. Spiritually speaking, they are "four" but not "four plus one." They do not have God and, thus, cannot work or bear responsibility. Today, we who have believed in the Lord Jesus and are saved have had a "one" added to us. The Spirit of God has entered into us, God Himself has entered into us, and His life has entered into us. Hence, we the created people have had God added to us. Since we have the life of God, we have become "five." We have become useful and can work and bear responsibility.

The Lord divided up the ten virgins into two groups of five, indicating that they had been created and had God added to them. They were saved and had God in them. Thus, they had to assume some responsibility. None of those who have been saved should receive grace in vain. Since we have received the grace to have God, and since God is now living inside of us, we should bear some responsibility before God. It is all right for the unbelievers, who do not have God, to live their lives in a loose and sloppy way. But it is not acceptable at all for us Christians who have gained God and have God inside of us to live loosely and sloppily. If a person is not saved and does not have God inside of him, although he may not be watchful, God may leave him alone. But if you are saved and have God in you as your life and strength, and yet you still live a sloppy life as the unbelievers do, then the Lord will come to warn you.

The Lord Requiring the Saved Ones
to Bear the Responsibility to Be Prudent Virgins

The Lord requires all of us who have been saved to bear a certain responsibility before God. What is this responsibility? It is to be a prudent virgin. Since we have been saved, we must bear the responsibility to choose whether we will be prudent believers or foolish believers. Whether we are foolish or prudent is under our control. God will not decide for us.

The Prudent Virgins Preparing Oil in Their Vessels

Some may ask what it means to be prudent. The Lord said, "For the foolish, when they took their lamps, did not take oil with them; but the prudent took oil in their vessels with their lamps" (Matt. 25:3-4). The Chinese Union Version uses the phrase *prepare oil* in its translation of this verse—"For the foolish, when they took their lamps did not prepare oil with them; but the prudent prepared oil in their vessels with their lamps." The foolish did not prepare, but the prudent did. Those who prepared were the prudent ones, and those who did not prepare were the foolish ones. What did the prudent ones prepare? They prepared the oil. Both the foolish and the prudent virgins took their lamps. The difference was that the foolish ones did not prepare oil in their vessels, while the prudent ones did. The prudent ones prepared oil not only in their lamps but also in their vessels. The lamp is one thing, and the vessel is another thing. This parable tells us that every virgin should have two portions of oil—one portion burning in the lamp and a second portion prepared in the vessel in addition to the portion in the lamp. This is similar to a car, which normally has a spare tire besides the four tires. The prudent virgins were truly prudent because they prepared oil in their vessels besides the oil in their lamps.

The Oil in the Lamp Signifying
the Regenerating Spirit

What do the oil in the lamp and the oil in the vessel refer to? The oil in the lamp signifies the regenerating Spirit. Therefore, the oil in the lamp does not need to be prepared. All ten virgins, both the foolish and the prudent, had oil in their lamps, which were all shining. What they still needed to prepare, in addition to the oil in their lamps, was oil in their vessels. Most people who know the Bible acknowledge that oil signifies the Spirit. When we are saved, the Spirit enters into us. This is the oil in the lamp. The oil in the lamp signifies the regenerating Spirit. When we are saved and receive the Lord as our Savior, we are regenerated, and the Spirit begins to live inside of us. From that time onward, the Spirit wants to shine forth from within us. This is the experience of every saved person. If someone does not have the regenerating Spirit in him, then he has not been saved yet. Every saved Christian has the Spirit of the Lord and the life of the Lord inside and thus is a genuine virgin with oil in his lamp.

The Oil in the Vessel
Signifying the Infilling Spirit

It is not enough to have oil merely in our lamps. It is not enough to have merely the regenerating Spirit. Besides this portion of the Spirit, we need to have another portion of the Spirit. The second portion of oil is not the oil in the lamp but the oil in the vessel. The Lord said this to show us that there are two different portions of the Spirit. The first portion is the regenerating Spirit that all believers gain when they are saved. However, after they are saved, they have to prepare themselves with the second portion of the Spirit, the infilling Spirit. We have the regenerating Spirit, but we may not necessarily have the infilling Spirit. Although we are saved, we may not be filled with the Spirit. We have the first portion of the Spirit, but we may not necessarily have the second portion of the Spirit. Although the Spirit is in us, it may not fill our entire being. Thus, although we are Christians, our condition may not be very vital because we may not have enough of the infilling Spirit. We may not have enough oil prepared in our vessels.

We have all believed into the Lord, are saved, and have the life of the Lord. However, I must ask you all whether you have the Spirit of the Lord. Perhaps some of you may say, "Thank the Lord, we all have the Spirit of the Lord." This is good. You have believed into the Lord and are saved, and you have the life of the Lord and the Spirit of the Lord. However, I want to ask whether or not you are fervent deep within. Some may say, "Although I am saved, inwardly I am lukewarm. I go to the movies, but I am not thrilled. I go to the meetings, but I am dispirited and discouraged. I am truly lukewarm." This is exactly the situation that the church in Laodicea was in.

Are you strong in the spirit? Do you have power in your gospel preaching? Are you released in the meetings? As a Christian are you full of joy and free? Many of you may answer, "I do not know why I am so weak. When I do not attend the meetings, I do not feel right inside. But when I go to the meetings, I feel bored and very depressed. I can neither open my mouth nor pray. I know that it is my duty to preach the gospel, but I do not want to do it. When I preach the gospel, I cannot speak much and I feel exhausted. I do not have any power. Originally, I thought it was a joyful thing to be a Christian, but I have been sad for a long time. I want to give up the Lord and stop being a Christian, but deep within I cannot get through. I want to be a good Christian, but I cannot make it." What kind of condition is this? This kind of condition indicates that "our lamps are going out" (Matt. 25:8). This means that there is a little bit of oil in our lamps, but there is no oil prepared in our vessels. In other words, we have been regenerated and we have the regenerating Spirit, but we are not filled with the Spirit. We have the regenerating Spirit but not the infilling Spirit.

When the Spirit fills our entire being, that is, when we gain the infilling Spirit, we cannot help but become hot. We cannot be cold anymore. Once the Spirit fills us, our inner being will be burning, and we will become hot. When we come to the meetings, we will be released. We will open our mouths to pray, praise, and testify. We will have power inwardly. When we preach the gospel and speak about the Lord Jesus to people, we will touch their feelings and will have the presence of the Spirit. Moreover, we will be filled with joy and peace deep within. We will be free from bondage and oppression.

For example, suppose there is a dear brother sitting in the meeting whose spiritual condition is like a lamp that is going out. He is weak, his spirit is depressed, and his inner being cannot be lifted up. When he talks about worldly matters, he is interested, excited, and has much to say. But when it comes to spiritual matters, he is uninterested and has nothing to say. If we are those who are full of the Spirit, then we will open our mouths to pray, sing, and praise. The burning fire in us will not allow us to be silent. In this way the majority of the saints in the meeting may be depressed, yet even though we are the minority, we can still make the meeting living and burning because we are filled with the Spirit. This will deliver us from the pitiful situation of being lukewarm, naked, poor, blind, and self-contented.

A CHRISTIAN'S MATURITY IN LIFE—
PURSUING THE FILLING OF THE SPIRIT

At the beginning of our salvation we have the regenerating Spirit and God's life and nature in us, but we do not have the infilling of the Spirit in us. We have oil in our lamps, but we do not have oil prepared in our vessels. We are shining, but the light in us may be going out. We are not mature in life.

What is the way to mature in life? The way to mature in life is to prepare oil in our vessels, that is, to pursue the infilling of the Spirit. How do we pursue the filling of the Spirit? First, we must realize that the Spirit is the realization of Christ and that Christ is the embodiment of God (2 Cor. 3:17; Col. 2:9). The Spirit in us is actually Christ in us and God in us. Therefore, the maturity in life is the growth of Christ in us, that is, our being occupied by Christ and filled with God. Hence, to be filled with the Spirit means that our entire being is occupied by Christ and filled with God. Our thoughts, preferences, views, insight, inclinations, choices, and everything are occupied by Christ and filled with God.

Before we are completely filled, our views are our own views, our thoughts are our own thoughts, our preferences are our own preferences, and our choices are our own choices. In other words, everything comes out of us. Christ does not have any ground in us. We love whatever we like, and we reject whatever we do not like. There is nothing of Christ's element in us, nor is there any ground for the Spirit. Our person remains intact. Although the Spirit is in us, He may be suffering and may not have any ground in us. Can we grow in this way? Can we mature, be made ready, and see the Lord? No, we cannot mature unless we are willing to pursue the infilling of the Spirit, allowing Christ to occupy every part of us and allowing God to fill our entire being. If we do so, then our whole being will be filled with Christ, and we will be mature and full-grown in life. We will be the same as Christ and will have His glorious image. Then we can meet the Lord.

Paying the Price to Buy

How can we experience the infilling of the Spirit? In the parable of the ten virgins the Lord Jesus used a very good word—*buy* (Matt. 25:9). In order to have oil in our vessels we must buy, and to prepare oil in our vessels we must buy. This means that we have to buy in order to have the infilling Spirit. We all understand that to buy something means to pay a price. No matter what we buy, we must spend money, that is, pay a price. To buy clothes, food, groceries, or anything else, we have to pay a price. Moreover, how much we pay determines what kinds of things we can buy. Ten dollars can buy you something valued at ten dollars, whereas ten thousand dollars can buy you something valued at ten thousand dollars. Likewise, we can never gain the infilling of the Spirit without a cost. The infilling of the Spirit requires the paying of a price.

We often see saints praying in pursuit of the infilling of the Spirit. This is right. We need to ask the Lord for this. However, please remember that we not only need to ask but also to buy. It is useless to merely ask for the infilling of the Spirit before God and not buy. We definitely need to pay a price. What is the price? Paul says in Philippians 3, "But what things were gains to me, these I have counted as loss on account of Christ. But moreover I also count all things to be loss on account of the excellency of the knowledge of Christ Jesus my Lord, on account of whom I have suffered the loss of all things and count them as refuse that I may gain Christ....Brothers, I do not account of myself to have laid hold; but one thing I do: Forgetting the things which are

behind and stretching forward to the things which are before,
I pursue toward the goal" (vv. 7-8, 13-14). Essentially, what
Paul was saying was, "I, Paul, am saved, and I am old now.
Furthermore, I am imprisoned in Rome. I have followed the
Lord for many decades, yet I am still forgetting the things
that are behind and stretching forward to the things which
are before. I am counting all things as refuse that I may gain
Christ." The price that Paul paid was the price of all things. In
return, what Paul received was Christ.

All the Things in Us Other Than Christ Being the Price

We are saved and Christ is now living in us. However,
we must ask ourselves how much of Christ we have enjoyed. I
am afraid that we have not enjoyed Christ that much,
because what is in us is not Christ but many other things
that in comparison are like refuse. What we are filled with is
our reputation, our prospects, the world, position, power, and
wealth. We are not filled with the Spirit and do not have
much Christ in us. According to the speaking of Paul, everything that is in us or in our hearts that is other than Christ is
the price that we must pay. Whatever is in us, in our hands, or
in our hearts that is not of Christ is the price.

For example, suppose a brother has a beautiful tie that he
loves very much. When he is loving his tie, his love toward the
Lord decreases, and there is less ground in him for Christ. At
this moment, his tie is the price. We love many things such as
our wife, husband, children, houses, and cars. When we love
these things, there is less ground, or perhaps no ground at all,
in us for Christ. At this moment, all these things are the price
we must pay. Some saints may say, "I certainly love Christ,
but I cannot put aside my career and my job." What we cannot
put aside is the price. Whatever replaces Christ, is a substi-
tute for Christ, or is even against Christ—whether it is our
reputation, position, knowledge, wealth, desires, or thoughts—
is the price. Paul said that he forsook everything and counted
them as refuse in order to gain Christ. Christ is the treasure,
and Christ was what Paul treasured. We have to be like Paul
to pay every price to gain Christ.

The problem today is not that we do not know our condition but that we are unwilling to pay the price. When we look at our knowledge, prospects, material possessions, and family, we treasure them and hold on to them. In this way, Christ is left out, the infilling of the Spirit departs, and our light begins to go out. Time is not in our hands. May the Lord have mercy on us to grant us the light and the power of life so that we may pay the price to buy. The Lord told the Laodiceans, "I counsel you to buy" (Rev. 3:18). To the lukewarm Laodiceans, the Lord spoke of buying three items—gold refined by fire, white garments, and eyesalve to anoint their eyes. Can you see the light? Do you know the things of the Lord? Are you clear about spiritual matters? If you are not, it is because your eyes have not been opened. If you want your eyes to be opened to see the light, you must pay the price to buy. If you are willing to pay the price, you will see.

Salvation does not require the paying of a price, but maturity does. To obtain the oil in the lamp does not require one to pay a price, but to obtain the oil in the vessel does. The regenerating Spirit is given for free, but to obtain the infilling Spirit requires that we pay a price. If we are even a little willing for the sake of the Lord to put aside some of our desires, prospects, knowledge, position, family, material possessions, career, views, perceptions, and all the other things related to us, then the Spirit will fill us up. The more we forsake, the more the Spirit will fill us. How much we forsake is how much the Spirit will fill us. We may use a glass of grape juice as an example. When you empty a little of the juice, the air will fill up the glass a little more. When you empty more juice, more air will fill the glass. When the glass is fully emptied, the air will fill up the entire glass.

Only when we pay the price can we then "buy" the infilling of the Spirit. How much of a price we pay determines how much of the infilling we will gain. As human beings we need to believe in Jesus, and once we have believed in Jesus, we need to mature in life. Therefore, no matter what condition we are in—strong or weak, uplifted or depressed—we do not have a choice. Because we are not only human beings but also are those who have believed in Jesus, we must reach maturity and have the infilling of the Spirit. If you are strong, you need the infilling. If you are weak, you need the infilling even more. If you are uplifted, you need to be filled. If you are depressed, you need to be filled even more. May the Lord have mercy on us that He would enable us to pay the price and to get ready by buying the oil so that we may be mature to meet the Lord.

CHAPTER EIGHT

THE WAY TO BE FILLED WITH THE SPIRIT— GIVING THE LORD THE GROUND

Matthew 25:12-13 says, "But he answered and said, Truly I say to you, I do not know you. Watch therefore, for you do not know the day nor the hour." The phrase *I do not know you* in verse 12 can also be translated as "I do not approve of you" or "I do not recognize you." As we know, the difference between the foolish virgins and the prudent virgins is a matter of whether or not they have prepared oil in their vessels. The oil in the lamp refers to the Spirit that we receive in regeneration, whereas the oil in the vessel refers to the infilling of the Spirit that we receive by pursuing after we have been saved.

THE NEED TO PURSUE THE INFILLING OF THE SPIRIT AFTER RECEIVING THE SPIRIT IN REGENERATION

Why does God want us to pursue the infilling of the Spirit after regenerating us, saving us, and giving us the Spirit? The reason is related to the ultimate purpose of God's salvation. The purpose of God's salvation in the universe is to work Himself into man and to mingle Himself with man. Thus, those who will go forth to God in the future are simply those who are being mingled with God today. Therefore, everything that we do today must be done by God mingling Himself with us. Only this has eternal value. God regenerated us because He wants to live in us. By regeneration He put His life into us, that is, He incarnated Himself into us so that He could live in us. The Bible mentions several times that God abides in us and that we should also abide in Him (John 14:17-20). Paul even says, "It is no longer I who live, but it is Christ who lives in me" (Gal. 2:20). Christ's living in us is God's living in us. Christ lives in us through the Spirit. The Spirit in us is actually Christ and God in us.

Today the Triune God, who is Christ, the Spirit, and God, is already living in us, but do we give Him the ground in us? For example, in a normal family the parents are the elders and have their proper place. However, some families are in a rebellious situation in which the son assumes the headship and seizes all the position in the family without giving any to his parents. The son may force his parents to live in a small room in the corner, or he may have full authority so that only what he says counts and the parents do not have any authority. In such a family, the parents still live in the family, but they do not have the parental position. Although the parents are the elders in the family, they cannot exercise their authority. The inward situation of many saints is like this. Although God lives in them, they have given God almost no ground. Although the Spirit has touched them inwardly many times, they still tightly hold on to their authority. This is our situation.

We sometimes go against the feelings of our conscience and extinguish the feelings that are in the deepest part of our being in doing things that usurp the authority of God. Although the Spirit is in us, most of the time we do not give Him the authority and thus do not have the infilling of the Spirit. Although we have been saved and have the life of God, we often do not give God the authority and consequently are not people filled with the Spirit. Thus, we need to pursue and be dealt with before the Lord. We do not need to pursue to receive the Spirit. Rather, we need to pursue to be dealt with so that the Spirit can gain us. The Spirit is already living in us, and we have already received the Spirit. However, most of us have not given ourselves to the Spirit and have not let the Spirit gain us. Although we belong to Christ today, most of us still live by ourselves and are our own masters. We do not live by Christ and do not let Christ be our Master. In a sense, we have "parents" in our family, but most of the time we do not let them be the masters and do not respect their authority. This is an abnormal situation.

DOING EVERYTHING ACCORDING TO
THE SPIRITUAL PRINCIPLE

For a human being, it would be very rebellious to be such a child in such a family. For a Christian, it is very unspiritual to be this kind of Christian. No matter what kind of person you are, you need to know the principle of being that kind of person. If you are a student, you should study. The principle of being a student is to focus on studying hard. If you do not study or work hard as a student, you are not doing what you are supposed to be doing and should feel ashamed of yourself. This is true not only for students but also for people with any kind of occupation. Whether you are a storeowner, boss, professor, or doctor, you must follow certain principles. Similarly, there is a principle for being a Christian. A wise person, no matter what kind of person he is, will behave according to the principle for the kind of person he is. It would be very foolish for him to overlook or to violate that principle.

THE PRINCIPLE OF BEING A CHRISTIAN BEING
TO PURSUE THE INFILLING OF THE SPIRIT

What is the principle of being a Christian? Why are we Christians? What is the purpose of being a Christian? If we truly want to be Christians and to be called Christians, yet we overlook and violate the principle of being a Christian, then we are the most foolish people in the world. The principle of being a Christian is to let Christ mature in us. A Christian is a person who belongs to Christ, who is filled with Christ, and who expresses Christ. To express Christ requires that we be filled with Christ, and to be filled with Christ requires that we be filled with the Spirit of Christ. This is the principle of being a Christian. We must follow this principle so that Christ within us may possess us, govern us, and control us. Our entire inner being, that is, our mind, emotion, and will—including our thoughts, views, insights, opinions, preferences, choices, and decisions—must be brought under the governing of Christ. We must give Christ the right to control us so that He may move freely in us and possess us.

To get to this stage, we must be filled with the Spirit who is the essence of Christ. Christ controls, possesses, and governs

us in and through the Spirit. Therefore, we must pursue the
infilling of the Spirit. This is the principle of being a Christian. Christians who do not live according to this principle do
not behave like Christians and do not live up to the standard.
To live up to the standard, a Christian must be subject to the
principle of the infilling of the Spirit. In the parable of the ten
virgins, the virgins' preparing oil in their vessels signifies our
pursuing the infilling of the Spirit.

THE WAY FOR A CHRISTIAN TO MATURE IN LIFE— PREPARING OIL IN HIS VESSEL

No other passage in the entire Bible is as clear as the parable of the ten virgins in Matthew 25 in telling us the way a
Christian matures after being saved. That way, which is the
principle of being a Christian, is extremely simple—it is to
prepare oil in his vessel. Those who prepared were the prudent ones, and those who did not prepare were the foolish
ones. As Christians, whether we are prudent or foolish in the
eyes of the Lord will be determined not by so many other
things but by the principle of whether we have prepared oil in
our vessels. Whether or not we will be with the Lord, feast
with Him, and participate in the heavenly joy with Him in the
kingdom age does not depend on so many other things but on
whether we have prepared oil in our vessels.

Many Bible expositors agree that to prepare oil in the
vessel is to be filled with the Spirit. There is no question that
we have been regenerated and saved and have the Spirit within
us. The only question now is whether we have prepared the
oil in our vessel and have the infilling of the Spirit. We may
make light of this or may overlook this matter before the
Lord, but the Lord wants us to realize that our situation
before Him today and our future destiny all depend on our
attitude in this matter. In other words, our future destiny
depends on whether or not we have the infilling of the Spirit.
Let us consider the following questions. Have we been saved?
Have we been regenerated? Do we have the life of the Lord,
and are we children of God? Do we have the Spirit of God in
us? I believe that we would all say yes to all of these questions.
However, if I were to ask whether or not we have given the

Spirit the ground or whether or not the Spirit has the authority in us, I am afraid that we would find it difficult to answer.

By giving the Spirit the ground and allowing the Spirit to
have the authority in us, we are preparing our vessels with
the oil. However, we have to admit that most of us have not
given the Spirit the ground and the authority to fill us. We
may have many reasons and excuses for not preparing our
vessels with the oil. We may not even have the heart to be prepared with the oil. As Christians, we are often foolish and
unwise. May the Lord have mercy on us to open our inner
eyes and to clearly show us that this is the way for a Christian to mature so that we would rise up to pursue the infilling
of the Spirit.

CHRISTIANS BEING ORDAINED
TO BE FILLED WITH THE SPIRIT

The fact that we are human beings is not something
decided by us. We cannot choose to be human beings when we
are happy and choose not to be human beings when we are
unhappy. The fact that we are human beings was something
decided by God. The authority is in God's hands. God created
us. It does not matter whether or not we like being human
beings or whether or not we know how to live as human
beings. If God wants us to be men, then we must be men. As
men we are told by God through the gospel that we must
repent and believe in the Lord Jesus or else we will perish.
There is no point in arguing about this because the universe
is not in our hands. We are not the Lord of the universe. The
universe is under the authority and ordination of God. God
made us as men, so we have to be men. Now, having made us
as men, He wants us to believe in the Lord Jesus. If we protest against this, we are being foolish. There is no way to
change God's decision and selection. If we are wise, we will
submit to Him and say, "Oh, God, this is good. If You want me
to believe in Jesus, then I will believe in Jesus. Hallelujah."
Then we will have peace and joy.

We cannot argue with Him about this because the universe
is His, and the authority is in His hands. After we become
Christians, He says to us, "You have become a Christian, and

you have a regenerated life, but you still have to prepare oil in your vessel." This is simply a matter of His authority. If we prepare our vessels with the oil, we will be at peace and the result will be good. If we do not prepare our vessels with the oil and instead protest against Him, He will remain unchanged. We may give eight, ten, or even a hundred reasons in opposing Him, but we will not have the "amen" and the peace in the deepest part of our being. Our whole being will be inwardly upset. No matter how many reasons we present to God, the inward "amen" and the sense of peace will be withheld from us. We may have many excuses, but our inner being will not be at peace.

A Christian who is at peace and is joyful and whose inner being is in harmony with his outer being must be pursuing the infilling of the Spirit. If a person is not pursuing the infilling of the Spirit, he will surely have no peace within. He may have many reasons for not pursuing and may continually mention these reasons to God, but his innermost being will not be at ease and will have no peace. Because his inner being is in disharmony with his outer being, he will not have the boldness to kneel before the Lord and to pray. The Spirit who lives in the deepest part of his being will not say "amen." He may try his best to deceive the Spirit or to bribe Him, but the Spirit can never be deceived or bribed. Because of his hardness and his many reasons, the Spirit may be silent for a while since the Spirit does not contend with man. After he has given up his reasons and finished his talking, the Spirit may come again and speak to him while he is sitting alone in the middle of the night. The words of the Spirit may be completely contrary to the reasons that he gave. Thus, he will be unable to do anything. No Christian can avoid this. As Christians, we have to mature, and we must be filled with the Spirit.

BEING PRUDENT AND PAYING THE PRICE
TO BUY THE OIL

Whether or not we agree with God or whether or not we are submissive to Him, we can never change Him because the authority is in His hands. There are three facts that we cannot change: first, the fact that we are men; second, the fact that as men we must believe in Jesus; and third, the fact that as believers we must mature. The authority to change these things is not in our hands. Some people commit suicide because they are unhappy that they are men. Actually, to commit suicide is the most foolish thing to do because it only causes one to perish more quickly. God wants us to be men, so we must obediently be men. God wants us to believe in Jesus, so we must obediently believe in Jesus. Having believed in Jesus, God wants us to mature, to pursue the infilling of the Spirit, and to prepare oil in our vessels. We must submissively say, "Amen. Yes, God, I am willing to do this." If we do this, we will be the prudent ones whom the Lord will praise.

Many people say that honest advice often grates on the ear. Although these words may be unpleasant to your ear, they are nevertheless important and faithful. I hope that we would receive these words. If we are Christians, we must be mature Christians, and we must prepare oil in our vessels. Never regard the parables given by the Lord Jesus as playful and insignificant stories. The Lord said that the prudent ones prepare oil in their vessels, whereas the foolish ones do not. He will come one day and these two kinds of people will have to meet Him. You and I will have to meet Him one day. How will you meet Him? This is a big question. We cannot guarantee how many years we will live on the earth, whether it will be ten, twenty, sixty, or a hundred years. No matter how many years we will be alive on the earth, we must prepare our vessels with the oil within the limited time. How do we prepare our vessels with the oil? We have to buy it. To buy the oil is to pay the price. We have to pay the price to prepare our vessels with the oil.

THE REAL SITUATION OF MAN—
THE LORD HAVING NO GROUND

Salvation and the life of God are given to us freely, but the infilling of the Spirit is not. To gain the infilling of the Spirit we have to pay the price. How much of the infilling of the Spirit we gain depends on how much of the price we pay. When we are shopping, the more we pay, the more we can buy, and the less we pay, the less we can buy. To have the infilling

대가를 지불하여 기름을 준비하는것은 그에게 근거를 주는것입니다 、

of the Spirit we need to pay the price. How do we pay the price? According to the principle, we pay the price by giving the Spirit the ground in us. Before we were saved, we lived in the world and were our own masters. We did not give the Lord any ground and did not care about His authority. Everything that we treasured was ours—our family, children, husband or wife, future, business, material possessions, education, statuses, and all the things we enjoyed. The Lord did not have any ground in us.

We did whatever we felt like doing and were not restricted. Some people are seriously fallen because they give the ground in themselves to gambling, movies, and dancing. They neglect their families and put aside their careers. They only want to dance, play mah-jongg, and watch movies. Inside such ones are all kinds of corrupt things. The more proper ones let their future, education, status, career, and family occupy their entire being. There is no ground for God in them, and the Lord does not have any authority in them. This was our situation before we believed in the Lord. Unfortunately, many of us who have believed in the Lord are still in this kind of situation today. The Lord still does not have any ground in us.

LEAVING EVERYTHING
TO GIVE CHRIST THE GROUND

In the Gospels the Lord repeatedly asked people to leave everything (Matt. 19:29; Mark 10:29; Luke 18:29), to sell all that they had (Matt. 13:44-46; Mark 10:21), and to deny the self to follow Him (Matt. 16:24). What the Lord meant was that if we want to become His disciples, follow Him, and gain Him as salvation, the first criterion is that we must leave everything. What does it mean to leave everything? It means that we do not allow anything other than the Lord to occupy us. We do not allow education, money, fame, career, family, or children to occupy us. We have to empty out our hearts for Christ. This is what the Lord Jesus meant. He wants us to leave everything to follow Him. He wants us to pour out everything in our inward being other than Himself so that our hearts can be empty for Him.

Some people have the misunderstanding that the Lord

wants us to leave and neglect our family, husband, wife, business, career, and everything. Actually, when the Lord told us to leave everything, He did not mean that we should no longer care for the necessities of life but that all these things must not have the ground in us or occupy us. All the ground in us should be given to Christ. For example, consider a saint who is a student. For him to leave everything does not mean that he should no longer study but that the matter of studying should no longer occupy his heart. His heart should be empty for Christ. Then the Christ in him will lead him how to study and how far he should go in his studies. His leading is always higher than our own seeking.

The Lord said in the Gospels that we should leave our parents, wives, and children. However, in the Epistles the apostles tell the parents to raise their children properly, the children to obey their parents, the husbands to love their wives, and the wives to be subject to their husbands (Eph. 6:1-4; Col. 3:18-21). Furthermore, they tell us to not only provide for our immediate family but also for our relatives. If we do not do this, we are worse than the unbelievers (1 Tim. 5:8). These verses show us that to leave everything does not mean to abandon everything and to care for nothing. Rather, it means that all these things no longer have the ground in us because the ground in us has been given to Christ.

When we have given Christ the ground, He will tell us that He will keep us on the earth to make us more superior and proper than we used to be. When He wants us to put aside our family, it does not mean that He does not want us to care for our family. He simply wants us to give Him the ground and to not be occupied by our family. When He is the Lord in us and gains the authority, He will strengthen us and make us even more able to bear the responsibilities of the family. As husbands, we will be the best husbands, and as parents, we will be the best parents. We will do everything well and properly, yet our families will not have the ground in us because our ground will have been given to Christ.

The source of all our problems lies in whether or not we are willing to give Christ the ground. Perhaps all the saints may say that they are willing because they all desire to be mature Christians. However, I am afraid that leaving everything may be such a big price that nobody would be willing to pay it. However, those who truly know the Lord know that the Lord whom we follow is not so cruel or harsh. Throughout the past two thousand years there have been many who loved the Lord and who suffered poverty and humiliation for His sake, but their enjoyment of the Lord was much deeper and fuller than that of other people. Madame Guyon is a good example. Everyone agrees that she truly loved the Lord. She was born and raised in a noble family. There were many maids who served her. She did not have to wash her own clothes or even comb her own hair. Materially, she was truly rich. However, these things did not have the ground in her, nor could they touch her.

There was a brother whose clothing was very valuable, but his clothing did not occupy him and was not his world. Under the natural arrangement of God, he had a certain status and position to live this kind of a life, but those things did not have any ground in him. He did not love the world. This is the principle of living in the world. On the contrary, someone who may be very poor may want this thing or that thing. This is to love the world. Therefore, those who are rich and have high statuses are not necessarily those who love the world. Twenty years ago there was a brother in northern China who was very poor indeed. He stood up in a fellowship meeting one day and said, "Brothers, we should not love money. We should never love money." He gave a message on not loving money, but nobody said amen. Why? It was because he did not truly know the meaning of loving money and not loving money. He came to me for fellowship one day and asked me how his message had been that day. I told him frankly, "Brother, when you have made a hundred thousand dollars or two hundred thousand dollars, then you can give the message again. Only then will you know the meaning of loving money and not loving money." The fact that we do not have money does not mean that we do not love money. I am afraid that money may have far more ground in us than in those who have eighty thousand or a hundred thousand dollars.

EMPTYING THE VESSEL FOR GOD TO COME IN

What is the meaning of leaving everything? It means that all the things that are necessary in life do not have any ground in us. Rather, the ground in us has been given to Christ. How should we deal with our children, our family, and our career? The Lord within us will show us. No one can tell others how to deal with these matters. Our lives, statuses, and situations may be different, but our hearts should be absolutely the same. The ground in us should be given to Christ.

It is actually relatively easy to abandon all the things in our lives and to not live by them. It is much more difficult to live by those things and yet not give them the ground. It is like living in a family but not giving the family the ground in us. How difficult this is! Some religions persuade people to abandon their families and even to abandon everything, because they believe that everything is vanity and that people no longer need anything. The Lord, however, does not want us to live such a life. Instead, He wants us to have a family but to not give the ground in us to our family. All the ground has to be given to Christ. At the same time, we must act according to the will of Christ to properly bear the responsibilities of the family.

A co-worker once said that our heart is like a Chinese medicinal patch. Whatever it is applied to, it sticks to that. Likewise, whatever our heart touches, it sticks to it. When it touches education, it sticks to education. When it touches business, it sticks to business. When it touches money, it sticks to money. When it touches our family, it sticks to our family. Someone may say, "If our heart is like this, then I do not want anything." However, the Lord will tell that one, "No, that is not the way of My salvation. In My salvation you should have a family, bear responsibilities, become a husband and a father, do business, have a career, and lead a proper life, but all these things should not have the ground in you." This is the price that we must pay. What is it to pay the price? It is to empty our vessel for God to come in. Every inch of ground in us has to be given to Christ. When we give Him the ground,

잊가을 지불하는것은 우리의 그릇을 비워서
하나님이 오시게 하는것 입니다.

we will have God in us, and we will have the infilling of the Spirit.

Some fifty years ago in a Western country, there was a group of saints who were pursuing the infilling of the Spirit. One of them was a sister who loved the Lord very much and who was also pursuing the infilling of the Spirit. She prayed and waited. Then she prayed and waited again. While she was praying and waiting there, she felt that she had given the Lord the ground in her. It seemed that the Lord could do whatever He wanted to do in her except deal with her hair. During that time in the West, the most fashionable way for a woman to arrange her hair was to set it very high, like a tower. This sister allowed the Lord to touch everything she had except her tower-like hair. When she had the feeling that the Lord wanted to deal with her hair, she told the Lord, "Lord, if You touch my money, I am willing to offer it. If You want me to deal with my sins, I am willing to do it. However, my hair is really an insignificant matter, so please leave me alone." We can see that this sister's hairstyle was not sinful, nor was she loving the world by having this hairstyle. Many sisters today cut their hair very short and do not consider that they are loving the world. The problem is that man likes to reason. Who can say that setting one's hair very high is loving the world, while cutting one's hair very short so that it looks like neither a man's nor a woman's is not loving the world? The question we must ask is, who has the authority? Is the authority over your hair in your hands or in the Lord's hands? Who is the master of your head—you or the Lord?

Our reasons may be very plausible, but the Lord never listens to our reasoning. In a sense, He is unreasonable. Our "lawsuits" with the Lord are always one-sided. There are no plaintiffs and defendants. There is only His side. Whatever He says, that is it. There is nothing to argue about. During a meeting, the sister mentioned earlier came and, kneeling down, cried out loudly, "Lord, why do You not answer my prayers? Why have You not filled me with the Spirit? Lord, I have been so desperate. I have been praying and waiting. Whatever You wanted me to do I did. Why have You not given me the filling of the Spirit?" Then the Lord asked her, "Have you done all that I asked you to do? What about your hair?" She was speechless. On that day she knelt down and pulled her high hair down. Then she received the infilling of the Spirit. Once her hair was subject to the Lord, she was immediately filled with the Spirit. This is to pay the price.

What the Lord wants is not our wealth, our time, and our everything. What He wants is for us to allow Him to question us about everything. The Lord is not so cruel that He would ask us for everything that we love. The Lord wants us to allow Him to go through everything and to allow Him to have the ground in everything. The Lord will not necessarily fight against us to take away all our material possessions. The Lord may even give us more enjoyment, but the question is whether we will give Him the ground. All things are His. If we truly want to enjoy Him and love Him, we have to give Him the ground. Then we will be satisfied and will receive the filling of the Spirit. The Lord cares not for your hairstyle but for whether or not He has the ground. When you decide on your hairstyle, the Lord cares whether He is in it or not. What the Lord is fighting for is His authority and ground. Are the authority and ground in your hands or the Lord's hands?

If we bring all these questions before Him and give Him the authority and ground, we are paying the price to "buy" Him. He will have the ground in us to fill us. Perhaps one day He will give us clothing that is much more beautiful than the clothing we wore in the past. The Lord is merciful to us. The question is whether we will completely give Him the ground in us. What is it to be a vessel? To be a vessel is to be empty within. Then the oil can be put into the vessel. In order to contain the oil, the vessel has to be emptied and has to give room for the oil. If the vessel has no space and is not empty, then the oil cannot be put in. We are vessels, and we have to be emptied for the Lord. This is to pay the price.

CHAPTER NINE

THE WAY FOR A CHRISTIAN TO MATURE IN LIFE— PAYING THE PRICE TO BUY THE OIL

Matthew 25:3-4 mentions two things that are absolutely different—one is the lamp and the other is the vessel. The difference between the foolish virgins and the prudent virgins does not concern their lamps but the contents of their vessels. The prudent prepared oil in their vessels while the foolish did not. Verse 7 says, "Then all those virgins arose and trimmed their own lamps." This verse mentions only lamps, not vessels. Then verse 8 says, "And the foolish said to the prudent, Give us some of your oil, for our lamps are going out." This verse proves that the lamps of the foolish virgins were burning but were soon about to go out. This also implies that there was no problem with their lamps. Instead, the problem was that they did not take oil in their vessels.

We have to pay attention to what the lamp, the vessel, the oil in the lamp, and the oil in the vessel signify. Then we will know what our problem is. Proverbs 20:27 clearly tells us, "The spirit of man is the lamp of Jehovah, / Searching all the innermost parts of the inner being." The lamp is the human spirit within us, and our spirit is the lamp of God. Jehovah has a lamp in us, which is the spirit in man. God searches every part of our inner being using this lamp. The parts of our inner being are the parts of the human soul.

THE OUTER MAN BEING THE SOUL AND THE INNER MAN BEING THE REGENERATED SPIRIT

Second Corinthians 4:7 says, "But we have this treasure in earthen vessels that the excellency of the power may be of

God and not out of us." The treasure in this verse is the life of God and the Spirit of life. The earthen vessel refers to our being. Verse 16 says, "Therefore we do not lose heart; but though our outer man is decaying, yet our inner man is being renewed day by day." The outer man is our natural man, our soul, whereas the inner man is our regenerated new man, our regenerated spirit. Thus, the vessel mentioned in the previous verse refers to our outer man, our soul. The treasure is the life of God, the Spirit of life, mingled with our inner man, our spirit. Therefore, our spirit has the life of God and the Spirit of God, and our outer man, our soul, is a vessel.

THE SPIRIT BEING THE GLORY

Second Corinthians 3:6 says, "Who has also made us sufficient as ministers of a new covenant, ministers not of the letter but of the Spirit; for the letter kills, but the Spirit gives life." Verse 8 says, "How shall the ministry of the Spirit not be more in glory?" Verse 6 mentions the Spirit, and verse 8 mentions glory. Verse 6 says that the ministers of the new covenant are made sufficient to be ministers of the Spirit through which man can have life. Then verse 8 says that there is glory in the ministry of the new covenant. Therefore, the Spirit and glory are closely related. Verses 16 and 17 say, "But whenever their heart turns to the Lord, the veil is taken away. And the Lord is the Spirit; and where the Spirit of the Lord is, there is freedom." Our turning our heart to the Lord is our turning to the Spirit. Whenever the veil is taken away, the Spirit works to set us free.

Verse 18 says, "But we all with unveiled face, beholding and reflecting like a mirror the glory of the Lord, are being transformed into the same image from glory to glory, even as from the Lord Spirit." This means that our being transformed into the image of the Lord is our being transformed from glory to glory. Our being transformed from glory to glory is also from the Lord Spirit. In other words, our being transformed from the Lord Spirit is our being transformed from glory to glory. Anyone who knows Greek should realize that this verse shows us that our transformation from glory to glory and our transformation from the Lord Spirit are the same thing. They are two matters that refer to the same matter. This proves that glory and the Spirit are one thing. John 7:39 says, "But this He said concerning the Spirit, whom those who believed into Him were about to receive; for the Spirit was not yet, because Jesus had not yet been glorified." This also proves that glory and the Spirit are related.

THE LORD REGENERATING US IN OUR SPIRIT

We have already seen that the way for us as Christians to mature is to let the Lord fill us in our being, that is, to let the Spirit of the Lord have the full ground in us. When the Lord regenerated us, His Spirit with His life entered into us. Thus, our spirit, which was originally deadened, became enlivened. We know that death is darkness. When the spirit is deadened, it is dark and without light. When the Spirit of God with His life entered into our deadened spirit, our spirit was made alive and became bright.

God's Spirit is God's life, even God Himself. God Himself is light, and God's life is also light. Therefore, when the Spirit of God with God's life enters into us, it is like a great, rich light entering into our spirit. This great and rich light enters into our spirit and brightens it, making it full of light. Our spirit is the lamp of God. The lamp is where the light is. Light is contained in a lamp and shines through a lamp. Our human spirit is the lamp of God. The Spirit of God with God's life is the great and rich light contained in our spirit, which is the lamp. The spirit in us is bright and shining. God shines out from our spirit into our being. The purpose of His shining out is that He would shine into all of our inner parts.

THE THREE PARTS OF THE SOUL—
THE MIND, EMOTION, AND WILL

We all know that our spirit is the deepest, innermost, and most central part of our whole being. Surrounding the center of our being is the circumference of our soul, which is our very person, our self. When we talk about what kind of people we are, we are referring to our soul. Our soul, which is our natural man, clearly consists of three parts. These three parts are the organs by which we think, like and dislike, and make decisions. The organ by which we think is our mind, the organ by which we like and dislike is our emotion, and the organ by which we make decisions is our will. When added together, these three parts or organs make up our outer man, our soul.

The Spirit of God with God's life shines out from our spirit, shining forth to every part of our soul. The deepest and most central part of our being is our spirit. When the Spirit of God with God's life entered into this spirit, this spirit began to shine and became bright. Formerly, this spirit was in darkness and was deadened. Now this spirit shines and has been made bright and alive because the Spirit of God with God's life has entered into it. However, this central part of our being is only one part of our being. Surrounding this central part is our outer man, our soul. This soul consists of three parts—the mind, emotion, and will. All of our thoughts and knowledge come from the mind, all of our likes and dislikes are from the emotion, and all of our decisions, plans, choices, and resolutions are determined in the will. When we talk about our person, most of the time we are referring to what we think about, what we love, and how we make decisions. These are the activities of our person.

Proverbs 20:27 says that this spirit, which is our deepest part, is the lamp of God. Jehovah God searches the inner parts of man through this spirit. According to psychology, the inner parts of man consist of the mind, emotion, and will. From the human spirit God uses His Spirit to shine forth, penetrate, and search every part of man. Therefore, this spirit is the lamp, and the light in this lamp is the Spirit of God and God's life. This light needs to shine forth into every part of the human mind, emotion, and will.

GOD AND MAN BEING MINGLED IN THE SPIRIT— THE FIRST STEP FOR A CHRISTIAN TO BE MATURED IN LIFE

What is the way for a Christian to mature in life? We have to say again that the central meaning and purpose of being a Christian is to allow God to mingle Himself with us. The beginning of our being matured in life is when God first mingles with us, that is, when His Spirit with His life enters into our spirit. This is the first step. At this point our spirit has the element of God and is mingled with God, and we are regenerated. Our spirit was in darkness and death before we believed in the Lord. Because our spirit was deadened, we had no feeling, and because it was in darkness, we could not distinguish between black and white or right and wrong. However, when God's Spirit with God's life entered into us, our spirit was made alive and bright. The fact that our inner being has been made alive and bright is proof that God's Spirit with God's life has entered into us.

Perhaps some may ask how they can tell whether they have been made alive and bright in their inner being. Someone who is dead has no feeling, but someone who is alive has feeling. Before we believed in the Lord and were regenerated, perhaps we did not feel wrong when we quarreled with our family. We had no feeling in our deeper part and were dead inside. When we grip and pinch a person a little bit, he cries out in pain because he has feeling. If he were a dead person, he would do nothing no matter how much we gripped and pinched him because such a person is dead and does not have feeling.

Formerly our spirit was dead. We did not feel that we were wrong when we did something wrong such as quarreling with others in our family and causing turmoil. This proves that our spirit was dead and had no feeling. However, one day we believed in the Lord and were regenerated, and our spirit became alive. How do we know that our spirit has become alive? In the past when we blamed others and spoke in anger, we had no feeling. Now, however, whenever we do these things, we feel as if we are being poked by a needle. We feel that there is something wrong, and we have a sense of pain. This proves that we have been made alive. However, this feeling may still be somewhat weak. Though we may be pricked and may have a sense of pain in our heart, we may still want to reason and quarrel with others. The more we quarrel outwardly, the more we sense the pain inwardly. One day we may quarrel with our family outwardly, but inwardly we may be being pricked until we cannot bear it anymore. Then the next morning we may confess to the Lord, saying, "Lord, I lost my temper with my family yesterday. I was truly wrong. What should I do?" The Lord may then lead us to deal with this before our family and to tell them, "I was wrong yesterday. I feel very sorry about that. The Lord has convicted me, and I have no peace. Please forgive me." What is this? This is the spirit in us being alive, bright, and full of feeling. When the spirit in us is bright, we can distinguish between black and white and between light and dark. By this we know that we have been regenerated and that the Spirit of God with God's life has been mingled with our spirit. In other words, God and our person have already begun to be mingled in our innermost part.

EVERY SAVED ONE HAVING THE MINGLING OF THE SPIRIT IN THEIR SPIRIT

God is the Spirit, and the Spirit is the anointing oil. When we have the Spirit of God in our spirit, we have the anointing oil. Today we have electric lamps that shine because of the electricity running through their bulbs. However, at the time the Lord Jesus spoke the parable of the ten virgins two thousand years ago, lamps shone because of the oil burning in them. We have seen that the lamp mentioned in Matthew 25 is our human spirit and that the oil that makes the lamp shine is the Spirit. This Holy Spirit is the realization of God and has the life of God. God Himself is light, and God's life is also light. This light is not given forth simply from the Spirit, the oil. Rather, the light that comes from the Spirit with God's life shines out through our human spirit. This oil can give forth its light only when it is in the lamp. We who are saved and regenerated have the Spirit in our spirit, that is, we have the oil in our lamps, and we have light.

The ten virgins, both the prudent and the foolish, are exactly the same in this respect—they all have oil in their lamps. In this matter we who are childish and immature are the same as the most mature ones such as the apostle Paul. Paul's spirit could shine because he had the Spirit of God, the anointing oil of God. In the same way, our spirit can also shine because we have God's Spirit, God's anointing oil. Thus, we

are all the same in the matter of the Spirit being in our spirit
and the shining oil being in our lamps.

THE VESSEL BEING BROKEN
SO THAT THE SPIRIT MAY FLOW OUT

Now we must ask a very serious question. We have the
Spirit in our spirit, but do we have the Spirit in our soul? Do
we have the element of the Spirit in our mind, emotion, and
will? The Spirit is in our spirit, but what about our soul?
Is the Spirit in our soul? We most likely have light or brightness only in the central, innermost part of our being, while
the other parts of our being may still be dark and without
light.

Our spirit is the lamp of Jehovah, and our soul is the
vessel. What does this vessel contain? It should contain the
Spirit mingled with our spirit. For instance, we have a glass
with grape juice in it. The glass is the vessel, and the grape
juice inside is the content. The grape juice is in the glass,
which is transparent. Revelation 21 tells us that the wall of the
New Jerusalem is composed of precious stones, yet it is transparent. Is our soul transparent like glass? Our soul may be
like a wooden cup that conceals what is contained inside. In
our thoughts, loves, and choices, we are like wood, which is
not transparent.

How do we deal with a cup that is not transparent and
that conceals its contents? We must make an opening in the
cup to see its contents. If there is light in a light bulb that is
transparent, then the light can come forth. But if the light
is in an iron box, then the light cannot come forth. What must
we do to let the light come out? We must destroy the iron box
or make a hole in it to let the light come forth. When the iron
box is broken, then the light can shine forth.

In many of us the light of God cannot be seen. Why? The
Spirit of God dwells in us, and we have been regenerated and
saved and have the Spirit of God as light in our spirit, yet our
outer man, including our thoughts, insights, loves, decisions
and determinations, remains absolutely intact. Because there
is no opening, God's light cannot shine forth. There is no way
for the Spirit of God who is in us to get out. It is as if we have

a sign inside of us that says, "This road is blocked." When God's Spirit wants to shine forth through our mind, we say, "Blocked!" When God's Spirit wants to shine through our decisions and choices, we also say, "Blocked!" We surround God's Spirit day by day. We confine the Spirit of God to the central part of our being, our spirit. All our thoughts, loves, and opinions are solely ours. God in us is entirely limited and surrounded by iron walls. He cannot come out even a little. God is inside us, but because our outer man remains absolutely intact, it does not have any openings to allow God to come out.

THE WAY FOR A CHRISTIAN TO MATURE IN LIFE— ACCEPTING THE BREAKING AND PAYING THE PRICE TO BUY THE OIL

The way for a Christian to become mature is to accept the breaking from God. Often God works in us and speaks to us through the speaking of the Spirit, the speaking of the brothers, the speaking in the Bible, and the prophecies and testimonies of the saints in order to shine upon us. However, if we do not care about His speaking, do not listen to Him, and do not even respond to Him, then, because He loves us, He will cut an opening or make a hole in us. He will break our mind, destroy our emotion, and overtake our will so that our whole being will be subdued. In this way, the light of God and the life of God will shine forth from our incomplete and broken being. When there are openings and cracks in our being, not only inwardly but also outwardly, immediately the light shines out from within us. The more the inward light comes out, the more mature we become. When the light comes out completely, we will be fully matured. Then the Spirit of God, the life of God, and God Himself will fill us completely, and God and we will be mingled together completely. Our whole being will be filled with God. We will not only have God in our spirit, but we will also have God in our mind, emotion, and will. In other words, we will have God in our whole being from our inner spirit to our outer soul. This is the way to mature in life, and this is why we have to pay the price to buy the oil.

The oil is the Spirit, who came into our spirit, our lamp, when we were regenerated and saved. This oil was freely given to us by God. We did not need to pay a price. Since then, the work of God has been to spread this oil from our spirit to our soul. He wants our soul to be filled with His Spirit. For this we need to pay a price. We have to drop the thoughts in our mind, the desires in our emotion, and the decisions in our will. This is the price that we must pay. What does it mean to pay the price? To pay the price is to drop all that we have. No matter what our thoughts, desires, and decisions are, we have to drop them all because our thoughts, desires, and decisions are always in conflict with the Spirit. They cannot be at peace with the Lord Jesus. We are always in our soul, that is, in our mind, emotion, and will, but God in our spirit wants to come out into our mind, emotion, and will. However, we always surround and hinder Him to insure that He stays inside. He is a living, moving, and almighty God. He wants to spread in us, yet we argue with Him and hinder Him. This is our situation.

If we struggle with God day by day, unwilling to lose, to drop, all that is in our soul, and to pay the price, then God has no way but to work from the outside and to deal with us through our circumstances. If He cannot win the battle with us from the inside, then He has no other way but to send the angels to deal with us from the outside. Perhaps our family may oppose us or we may have some problems at work or sickness in our body. Sometimes it may seem that God is using all the armies of the devil to attack us until we are torn down. Do not reject God's discipline. God does not discipline the unbelievers in this way. Those whom God loves, He surely disciplines. Because God loves us, is merciful toward us, and wants us to be His glorious vessel, He has to break our iron walls. In order to transform us into a transparent vessel, He has to discipline us.

THE SPIRIT IN OUR SPIRIT SPREADING
INTO OUR SOUL FROM GLORY TO GLORY

If we accept His discipline, we will be bright and transparent people. Our thoughts will be like His thoughts, our love will be like His love, and our decisions will be like His decisions. When people meet us, they will feel that they are meeting God. We will have the taste of man and also the taste of God in us. We will be the mingling of God and man. Not only so, we will have the element of God in us. We will be transformed into God's image, that is, transformed from glory to glory (2 Cor. 3:18). What is this glory? This glory is the Spirit. When the Lord Jesus was glorified, the Spirit came (John 7:39). Glory is the manifestation of God, and the Spirit is also the manifestation of God. When we have the Spirit in us, we also have glory. In our spirit there is God's Spirit, who is also glory.

Even though we have the Spirit of God in us, who is glory, this glory has not been manifested because it is only in our spirit and has not yet been manifested in our soul, our outer man. Second Corinthians 3:18 says that we "are being transformed into the same image from glory to glory, even as from the Lord Spirit." This means that our transformation into the image of the Lord is the result of the Spirit spreading into our soul. Our transformation is from glory to glory—from the inner glory, that is, from the Spirit being in our spirit, to the outer glory, that is, the Spirit being in our outer soul. When we are transformed from glory to glory, or from the Spirit to the Spirit, we will have the Spirit both in our spirit and in our soul, both within and without. We will be transformed into the image of the Lord, even as from the Lord Spirit.

THE NEED TO ULTIMATELY PAY THE PRICE
TO BUY THE OIL

Therefore, whenever there is a struggle in our mind, emotion, or will, we have to drop all that is in our soul and pay the price to let the Lord win. Once we submit and lay down ourselves, the Lord will win, and we will gain the Spirit. This is what is meant by paying the price to buy the oil. At every time and in all matters, whenever we struggle with the Lord in our thoughts, preferences, and decisions, we have to be subdued, admit defeat, and lay ourselves down in order to let the Lord win and to let the Spirit spread out. In this way we will have the Spirit in our soul. This is the way to prepare oil in our vessel.

First, we are regenerated and have the Spirit in our spirit. The Spirit is in the lamp of Jehovah; in other words, we have the oil in our lamp. Gradually, we become mature and the Spirit spreads from our spirit to our soul that we may have the oil in our vessel. This is the preparation that we need after salvation. Only transformed and matured people can meet the Lord and be co-kings with the Lord.

In the parable of the ten virgins, the virgins woke up and trimmed their lamps when the bridegroom came at midnight (Matt. 25:6-7). This means that whether they were foolish or prudent, the first thing that they paid attention to after their resurrection was their spirit. This is the meaning of the phrase *trimmed their own lamps.* By that time, the foolish virgins discovered that they had not received sufficient dealings with their person and that in their soul, their vessel, there was a lack of the Holy Spirit and of the element of the oil. They still had to pay the price and go to those who were selling oil in order to buy the oil. This is the parable of the virgins. It shows us the way for a Christian to mature in life. May the Lord have mercy on us that we may prepare the oil in our vessel while we still have time.

CHAPTER TEN

THE WAY FOR A CHRISTIAN TO MATURE IN LIFE— TURNING OUR HEART TO THE LORD

In 2 Corinthians 3:16-17 Paul says, "But whenever their heart turns to the Lord, the veil is taken away. And the Lord is the Spirit; and where the Spirit of the Lord is, there is freedom." Paul says here that whenever our heart turns to the Lord, the veil is taken away. Who is the Lord? Who are we actually turning to when we turn to the Lord? Paul tells us in verse 17, "And the Lord is the Spirit; and where the Spirit of the Lord is, there is freedom." Verse 18 continues to say, "But we all with unveiled face, beholding and reflecting like a mirror the glory of the Lord, are being transformed into the same image from glory to glory, even as from the Lord Spirit."

OUR MATURITY IN THE CHRISTIAN LIFE DEPENDING ON OUR BEING FULL OF GOD INWARDLY

According to the Bible our spirit is the lamp of God (Prov. 20:27), and our soul is a vessel for God (Matt. 25:3-4). When we were saved, the Spirit of God as the oil entered into our spirit. Now God's desire is to have His Spirit worked more and more into the different parts of our soul. When every part of our soul is filled up with the Spirit of God, then we will be mature in the spiritual life. The maturity in spiritual life depends on our being inwardly filled up with God's element. God's unique goal for us and His unique work on us are to work Himself and to mingle Himself into our being. Although God has done many things in us to which He wants us to take heed, His unique, central, and primary task in us is to cause our being to be filled up with God's element, that is, to be filled up with God Himself.

The first step of God's work is that when we are saved, His Spirit enters into our spirit. From that time onward, His intention is that His Spirit, which is His element, would spread from our spirit to the various parts of our being. When He has completely worked Himself into every part of our being, then we will be mature in the spiritual life. Then we can meet the Lord with boldness because by then whatever the Lord is, we also will be (1 John 3:2). Just as the Lord is God mingled with humanity and humanity brought into God, we also have God being mingled with us and are being mingled into God. Inwardly and outwardly, the condition of our entire being will match and be in harmony with the Lord's. At that time, we will be able to meet and dwell with the Lord in glory.

PAYING THE PRICE TO HAVE OUR SOULS
FILLED BY THE SPIRIT

It is the work of God's free grace that the Spirit enters into our spirit. This work does not require us to do anything, nor do we need to pay a price for it. As long as we confess in our heart that we are sinners and open ourselves to receive Him as our Savior, the Spirit of God will enter into our spirit without any cost to us. However, from that time on, in order for the Spirit to work Himself into the various parts of our soul, we need to cooperate and pay the price. Why is it necessary for us to pay the price? It is necessary because various parts of our soul have been fully occupied by all kinds of people, matters, and things. The mind, emotion, and will of our soul are full of our natural concepts, thoughts, preferences, and choices. We love our reputations, positions, and money. We love our wives, our children, and ourselves. Our hearts have been filled up with our own desires. This makes it difficult for the Spirit to work Himself into our soul.

How can the Spirit work Himself into our mind if we are not willing to lay down the thoughts in our mind? How can the Spirit work Himself into our emotion if we are not willing to give up what we desire in our emotion? Likewise, if we are not willing to surrender our own choices in our will, there is no way for the Spirit to be wrought into our will. We know that our soul is a vessel composed of three parts—the mind, emotion, and will. Each of these three parts is itself a small vessel. The vessel of our emotion should be filled with the Holy Spirit, yet we allow other things to occupy our emotion. Even before the Spirit enters into our emotion, our emotion has already been filled up with so many other things. What our emotion loves are the things and matters that our emotion is filled with and occupied with. Consider the following questions. We are saved, but how many things other than the Lord are still in our emotion? If these things that are apart from the Lord have filled up our emotion and are occupying it, do you think that it is possible for the Holy Spirit to fill up our emotion?

In order for the Spirit to spread from our spirit to our emotion, we have to pour out all that is occupying our emotion. This pouring out is the paying of the price. For example, a glass may be used to illustrate our emotion. The grape juice that fills the glass symbolizes the desires that fill our emotion. If we want to fill up this glass with air, the only way to do this would be to pour out the grape juice. The more the grape juice is poured out, the more the air can fill the glass. Further pouring out of the grape juice will allow further filling up of the air. When the grape juice is completely poured out from the glass, the air will fill up the entire glass. Therefore, the problem is not that the air is not filling up the glass but that other things are occupying the glass. The Spirit is like the air. Only when we empty ourselves completely can the Spirit fill up our entire being.

THE SPIRIT BEING UNABLE TO FILL US BECAUSE OUR MIND, EMOTION, AND WILL DO NOT HAVE THE LORD

Today the problem is not with the Spirit's infilling but that many things apart from the Lord are occupying us. From morning to evening, our emotion desires many things that, though they may not be evil, filthy, or sinful, are not the Lord Himself. The grape juice may be good because it contains ingredients such as water and sugar, yet the grape juice is not the air. Our desires may be good, proper, and noble, yet these things are not the Lord Himself.

Ever since He saved us, the Lord has been continuously working to move us, demand of us, encourage us, and even wait for us to empty out the things that are occupying our emotion so that He can have the ground. However, what is our response? The Lord repeatedly touches us, and we are touched, but we do not move. The Lord repeatedly makes requests of us, but although we hear Him, we do not answer Him. Do we not realize that the things that we love and desire are not the Lord? Do we not realize that the Lord has been wrestling in us with the things that we desire? Sometimes we bargain with the Lord until He gives in. Even when we agree to the Lord's requests, eventually we still break our promises.

Many times we encounter frustrations and difficulties that we cannot overcome. At those times we may yield to the Lord, saying, "O Lord! You are asking too much from me. Please reduce Your demand a little." Our Lord is not cruel and will sometimes go along. Then we may have an inward sense of peace, and we may tell the Lord, "Lord, the difficulties are gone, and I want to love You more." However, as time goes by, does our being change? What happened to our promises to the Lord? We are indeed unfaithful. Our emotion is still occupied by the matters that occupied us before. We still shut the door on the Lord, leaving Him outside the door. Our condition is like that of the church in Laodicea. Although we love the Lord and consistently pray and attend the meetings, we are not willing to practically pay a price, and in the end we become lukewarm. The Lord has no ground in us and has been shut outside the door by us, the lukewarm Laodiceans.

In Revelation the Lord says, "Behold, I stand at the door and knock; if anyone hears My voice and opens the door, then I will come in to him and dine with him and he with Me" (3:20). The Lord desires to have mutual enjoyment with us. Even though He is in our spirit, we often shut Him outside the door. We shut Him outside the door of our emotion. Our spirit is like a refrigerator in which we keep the Lord. Therefore, the Lord has no way to enter into our inner chambers and into our heart. The Lord is standing and knocking in our cold spirit, longing to enter into our heart and our emotion, yet our heart remains so hard and cold.

Not only is our emotion like this, our mind is even more so. The Lord has hardly any ground in our mind. Our mind is filled with many things other than the Lord. Once a brother in Shanghai told a story concerning our mind. He said that there was a sister attending a meeting in which a brother was giving a message. This brother asked the sister how many chapters were in the Gospel of Matthew. She said that there were thirty-eight chapters. He then asked her how many chapters were in the Gospel of Mark. She replied that there were twenty-six chapters. The brother went on to ask her how many of her clothes were blue and how many were red. She answered that she had exactly five items of clothing that were blue and three that were red. This sister knew the number of clothes she had that were blue or red, but regarding the number of chapters in the Gospels of Matthew and Mark, her memory was confused. Her confusion in this regard indicated where her mind was. Since her mind was so occupied with her clothing, how could there be room reserved for the Lord? If our mind is like a glass that is fully occupied, how can the Lord occupy even a small part of it? Since we have been saved by grace, our thoughts and considerations may not be evil. However, neither are they the Lord Himself. In our mind we are continually thinking, calculating, and planning. We are unable to stop thinking for even a second. Only we ourselves know what we are thinking about.

What is our response when the Spirit touches us, enlightens us, gives us a feeling, or makes a request of us? We may still try to bargain with the Lord. Is this the way to give ground to the Spirit? No, when the Spirit makes a demand on us, we should immediately pay the price, lay down our opinions and desires, and deal with and get rid of all these things. To deal with and get rid of these things is to pay the price. This is the case not only with our emotion and mind but also with our will. How many of our opinions, decisions, and selections are of the Lord? The decisions we make in our will are mostly made for ourselves. Thus, the Spirit cannot fill us, and the

Lord cannot spread into the three parts of our soul—our mind, emotion, and will. This is because our soul has been fully occupied by ourselves, not the Lord.

THE WAY FOR A CHRISTIAN TO MATURE IN LIFE

Turning Our Heart to the Lord and Having the Veil Taken Away

What is a mature Christian like? The deepest and inner-most part of our being is our spirit. One day the Lord entered into our being. His entering in was actually the entering in of the Spirit of the Lord. Our spirit was then filled with the Lord, and we were regenerated. This happened in our innermost part, the center of our being. Now we have the Lord who is the Spirit inside of us. When we receive the Lord, we receive the Spirit and are regenerated. For this we do not need to pay a price. We simply receive Him by believing. However, our outer man, which is our soul composed of three parts—our mind, emotion, and will—has been filled with ourselves and the things of the world. Our mind, our emotion, and our will are filled with ourselves and the things of the world. Can the Lord enter into our soul when it is in such a condition? He cannot. The Spirit of the Lord in our spirit would like to spread outward, yet our soul has fenced Him off, restricting Him in every way. Thus, He is unable to touch us and move into our soul. When the Lord touches us, we are touched, but we do not move. This is the reason why the Spirit is unable to fill us up.

Second Corinthians 3 gives us the way to break through this situation. "But whenever their heart turns to the Lord, the veil is taken away. And the Lord is the Spirit; and where the Spirit of the Lord is, there is freedom" (vv. 16-17). We saved ones all have the Lord who is the Spirit in our spirit. There-fore, the Lord and we are very closely joined. There is no distance between the Lord and us. Nevertheless, why does it often seem that the Lord is not so near and accessible to us? This is because there is a veil between the Lord and us. When we were regenerated, the Lord entered into our being and dwelt in our spirit. At that time we were face to face with the

Lord, fellowshipping with Him. However, as we faced the people, matters, and things in our daily life day after day, we unconsciously turned away from the Lord. This turning away is the veil.

Paul said that whenever our heart turns to the Lord, the veil is taken away. This veil is neither a matter nor an event but our turning away from the Lord. Suppose a brother and I are very close together and are facing each other. However, if I turn away from him, even though I am still very close to him, I cannot see him. This is the meaning of having a veil. My turning away from this brother is the veil. However, when I turn toward him again, this veil is taken away, and we can behold each other again. It is the same with the Lord who is in us. He is near to us in our spirit. In the beginning, the Lord and we were face to face. However, our hearts did not love Him that much and turned away from Him, facing our children, studies, reputations, positions, and money instead. When our heart pursues the things in the world and not the Lord, a veil comes between the Lord and us.

The heart is a very special part of our being. It has the component of the conscience and also the components of the mind, emotion, and will. For instance, self-condemnation in the heart issues from the function of the conscience, the desires of the heart issue from the function of the emotion, the considerations in the heart issue from the function of the mind, and the decisions made in the heart issue from the function of the will. Therefore, the mind, emotion, and will all rest upon the heart. In other words, the heart is connected with the mind, emotion, and will and is also connected with the spirit because the conscience is a part of the spirit. In view of this, the heart is a master switch, a key control point in man's inner being. Everything must go through the heart. Nothing can go through us unless it goes through our heart.

The heart is like an electric switch. When an electric switch is turned on, electricity is supplied. When the electric switch is turned off, the supply of electricity is terminated. In our spirit is the Spirit, which is the electricity, and our heart is the electric switch. Unless the heart is "turned on," the Spirit cannot come out and reach our mind, emotion, and will. How can the heart be turned on? It must be turned toward the Lord. The Spirit cannot enter into our emotion because our heart is not turned toward the Lord. The Spirit cannot enter into our will because our heart is not turned toward the Lord. To turn to the Lord is to love Him. When our heart turns to the Lord, we will love Him. When we love Him, we will spontaneously be open to Him. When we are open to Him, there will be no more veils. Before, our heart was turned away from Him, did not love Him, and was not facing Him. Now our heart has been turned around. When we turn our heart around, there is no more veil, and we can behold the Lord face to face.

We have the Lord in us, and we have the Spirit of the Lord in us, but we and the Lord are often not in fellowship each day. Why? This is because our heart is not turned toward the Lord and because we love other things and not the Lord. We realize that the Lord is in us, yet we do not love Him. We do not want the Lord and do not turn to Him. Thus, our heart is turned away from Him, and a veil comes between the Lord and us. However, once our heart turns around to be face to face with the Lord, the veil is taken away. At this time, our heart is open and the Spirit can spread out from our spirit into our emotion through our heart. Through our heart the Spirit can also spread to our will and to our mind. The more we love the Lord, the more our heart will open to the Lord and the more the Spirit will enter into our emotion. Also, the more we love the Lord, the more the Spirit will enter into our mind and our will. The more we turn to the Lord and the more we love Him, the more the Lord will have a way to spread out from our spirit through our heart into every part of our soul.

Beholding the Glory of the Lord
with an Unveiled Face

In 2 Corinthians 3:18 Paul says, "But we all with unveiled face, beholding and reflecting like a mirror the glory of the Lord, are being transformed into the same image from glory to glory, even as from the Lord Spirit." This verse indicates that when our heart turns to the Lord, the veil will be taken away, and we will behold the glory of the Lord with an unveiled face. For instance, sisters love to beautify and adorn themselves. This desire to beautify themselves issues from the function of their emotion. When they think about the different things and ways to beautify themselves, their mind is functioning. As they decide what cosmetics to buy, their will is functioning. Because of this matter of beautification, their entire soul is functioning. This kind of soul, which consists of the mind, emotion, and will, does not have the Lord. Many sisters confine the Lord in their spirit. Even as they pray, they tell the Lord, "Lord, let me beautify myself this time. There is a special need this time, so please let me do it this one time." What is the outcome? The outcome is that they can no longer fellowship with the Lord because there is a veil. As their heart turns away from the Lord, He has no way to get through them. It is as if He were hitting a brick wall or being shut outside the door.

For example, suppose a sister is moved by the Spirit of the Lord and responds to His love, saying, "Lord, although I love to dress up and live to adorn myself, I love You even more. I turn my heart and face toward You." Once she turns to the Lord in this way, the veil will be taken away. Immediately, she will be face to face with the Lord and will behold the Lord and the glory of the Lord. As her emotion turns, she will begin to love the Lord. She will then realize in her mind that such beautification is not after the Lord's desire, does not glorify the Lord, and is not pleasing to the Lord. Then she will pray to the Lord, "Lord, if this is the case, then I am willing to lay down and surrender my views and opinions. Lord, what You like is what I like, and what You consider good, I also consider good." The Spirit of the Lord will thus come out from her spirit through her heart to her emotion and to her mind. Then she will be able to declare boldly, "Lord, by Your grace I would not beautify myself in this way and would not purchase these kinds of clothing anymore." Thus, the Spirit will also move into her will through her heart.

If in every matter in our daily living our heart would be open and turned to the Lord, allowing Him to pass through and allowing the Spirit to enter into every part of our soul, then our mind, emotion, and will would be filled with the

Spirit. But for this we have to pay the price, yield ourselves, and surrender ourselves again and again. This repeated sur-rendering and yielding is the paying of the price to buy the oil, that is, the paying of the price to be filled with the Spirit. The more our soul is filled up with the Holy Spirit, the more mature in life we will become.

Reflecting like a Mirror and Being Transformed into the Image of the Lord

Whether or not we become mature in life depends on whether or not our heart loves the Lord. If our heart turns away from the Lord, He will be bound in our spirit and will have no way to come out or spread out. One day, however, the Lord may touch us, and our heart may turn back to Him. Through the turning and opening of our heart to the Lord, we are able to behold the glory of the Lord face to face. As we behold the Lord day after day in all our situations, we will eventually reflect the Lord's glory and be transformed into His image from glory to glory. In other words, if we open to Him a little today, then we will see something of Him today. If tomorrow we open to Him further, then tomorrow we will see something more of Him. We are like a mirror and an unveiled face aimed at Him. The more we focus on Him and draw near to Him, the clearer and more glorious our reflection of His glory will be.

What is the meaning of an unveiled face? An unveiled face is a heart that is turned to the Lord. If I turn my back to a person, I would not have an unveiled face to him. However, when I turn and face him, my face is an unveiled face to him. Likewise, whenever our heart loves the Lord and turns to Him, our heart and our face toward Him are unveiled. We can then behold Him face to face and fellowship with Him every day. The Lord through His Spirit will fill our being—our mind, emotion, and will—with His glory and with Himself as the Spirit. Consequently, whatever we think about, love, or choose will have the Lord's image because they will all have the Lord's element. Then we will be mature.

HAVING FREEDOM AND GLORY

There are two characteristics of someone who is mature in the Christian life. One characteristic is that he has glory, and the other is that he has freedom. When the Lord through His Spirit works His glory, which is Himself as the Spirit, into us and saturates us from our spirit into the three parts of our soul, then we are becoming mature in life from glory to glory. Eventually, our entire inward being will be glory. Our mind, our emotion, and our will will be glory. Our entire being will be glory. Not only so, our entire being will be free. There will be no more bondage in our mind, emotion, and will. There will be no bondage from our spirit to our soul. Every part of us will be set free.

Based on our experience, we can all testify that anyone who loves something other than the Lord not only binds up the Lord but also becomes bound himself. For instance, many sisters love to beautify themselves, with the result that the Lord has no ground in them to move. As a result, they themselves are also under bondage and have no freedom. Those brothers who love their future will be in the same situation—the Lord will be bound, as will they. Only when we are willing to pay the price and to lay down whatever the Lord wants us to lay down will our heart turn to the Lord. Then He will gain the ground in us and will be able to freely operate in us. We will also be released and will have freedom. Then when people touch us, they will sense a taste of the Lord. This is to have the image of the Lord. May our heart turn to Him.

CHAPTER ELEVEN

THE WAY FOR A CHRISTIAN
TO MATURE IN LIFE—
TURNING TO THE SPIRIT

Second Corinthians 3:16-17 says, "But whenever their heart turns to the Lord, the veil is taken away. And the Lord is the Spirit; and where the Spirit of the Lord is, there is freedom." Verse 16 says that the heart needs to turn to the Lord, and then verse 17 says that the Lord is the Spirit. This means that the heart needs to turn to the Spirit. Moreover, the phrase *where the Spirit of the Lord is, there is freedom* means that the Spirit of the Lord Himself is freedom. Because the Spirit of the Lord is freedom, where the Spirit of the Lord is, there is freedom. Then verse 18 continues, "But we all with unveiled face, beholding and reflecting like a mirror the glory of the Lord, are being transformed into the same image from glory to glory, even as from the Lord Spirit." An unveiled face is a face without any veils, and a veiled face is one that is covered by a veil. According to this verse, when the heart turns to the Lord, the veil is removed. Moreover, when the face is unveiled, it can behold the glory of the Lord. When we behold the glory of the Lord, we become like a reflecting mirror, and we are transformed into the image of the Lord from glory to glory. Our being transformed into the Lord's image is from glory to glory, even as from the Lord Spirit. The Lord is the Spirit, the glory is the Spirit, and the Spirit is the Lord. Hence, to be transformed into the Lord's image "from glory" is the same as to be transformed into the Lord's image from the Lord and also the same as to be transformed into the Lord's image from the Spirit.

THE WAY TO MATURE IN LIFE

We all know that the purpose of God's salvation is to work in us so that we may have His image (Rom. 8:29). How does this relate to being mature? To be mature is to have the Lord fully formed in us. It also means that we, those who have been saved, have been fully transformed into the Lord's image. Originally, we are men who are merely natural—not having the life of the Lord, the nature of the Lord, or the image of the Lord within us. However, through the salvation of the Lord, the Lord has added Himself into us. Since the time of our regeneration and salvation, the Lord has been adding Himself into us, causing us to have His life and nature. In other words, from the time of our salvation, the Lord has been working in us that we may have His image. When the Lord has fully worked His image into us and is fully expressed out from within us, then we will be mature in life.

THE DIFFERENCE BETWEEN
THE SAVED AND THE UNSAVED BEING THAT
THE SAVED HAVE GOD'S ELEMENT IN THEIR SPIRIT
AND THE UNSAVED DO NOT

What is the way to become mature? We all know that when we were regenerated, God put His Spirit and His life into our spirit. His purpose in doing this is to make us the same as He is, having His life and nature. When He makes us completely the same as He is, we are mature in life. How does the Lord do this? The first step that the Lord takes is to put His Spirit and His life into the deepest and most central part of our being—our spirit—at the time of our salvation. Thus, we have the Lord's Spirit, the Lord's life, and the Lord's element in our spirit. This is the difference between a person who is saved and a person who is not saved. A person who is saved has God's Spirit and God's life in his spirit. The difference between a saved person and an unsaved person is not related to outward appearance but to whether they have an extra element in the depths of their being. This element is God, the Spirit of God, and the life of God.

For example, suppose that there is a person who has not been saved, yet who was born with a very good nature and is a very proper person. This person does not have God's Spirit or God's life within him; he is merely a good person. Suppose, however, that there is another person who was not born with a good nature, who has a bad temper, and who is not a nice person. Suppose also that this person repented and received the Lord Jesus as his Savior and that the Spirit of God and the life of God entered into him. If you look at the outward appearance of these two people, you might be amazed. Although one is good and the other is bad, the good one is not saved but the bad one is. The difference between the two of them is not outward but is something within. The one who is good yet is unsaved does not have the life of God or the Spirit of God, whereas the one who is outwardly bad yet is saved has God's Spirit and God's life within him.

GOD TRANSFORMING MAN
THROUGH HIS SPIRIT AND LIFE

Some may think that if a person who is outwardly bad gets saved by God's Spirit and life, he should endeavor to have good behavior and conduct. However, this is merely self-cultivation, which is the work of a religious person. God does not save us in this way—He does not correct our shortcomings from the outside. God saves us by causing His Spirit and life to expand and spread out from our spirit, our inner being, so that we are completely changed. After a person who has a bad nature receives God's Spirit and life, God desires that His Spirit and life would spread out from within this person until he is completely swallowed up and transformed. Man's way is to outwardly improve and correct himself; God's way is to swallow us up and transform us from within. What is the basic material that God uses for this transforming work? The basic materials that He uses are His Spirit and life.

NOT OUTWARD IMPROVEMENT BUT
INWARD TRANSFORMATION

Throughout the ages, the aim of the teachings of the great theologians and philosophers has been to improve, reform, and beautify people outwardly. However, this is not the way of God's salvation. The way of God's salvation is to put His divine life into man's spirit to regenerate man. Then God causes His divine life to spread out from man's spirit to saturate and permeate him. We can liken this to putting yellow liquid into the center of a cotton ball. If we do this, then the yellow liquid will slowly flow and permeate out from the center. Eventually, it will saturate the whole cotton ball, causing the white cotton ball to become yellow. This yellow color does not come from outward painting but from inward saturation. This is the same way that a Christian becomes mature in life.

A saved person may have a fiery disposition and a bad temper, but on the day that he got saved, the Spirit of the Lord and the life of the Lord entered into his spirit. If from that day on he truly loves the Lord and is willing to give the Lord the opportunity to do the work of permeation in him, the Lord will permeate him to the extent that his temper will be changed. His naturally fiery temper will become gentle and will gain a little of God's "color." Then the Lord will continue to permeate him. As a result, although he was not a man with sympathy before, he will now have a heart to care about others, and will have a little bit more of God's color. These changes will not happen as a result of outward reform or from an outward painting of color onto him. They will happen as a result of the expansion and permeation of God's life within him. We can say that when this man first got saved, he was merely saved. His temper had not been changed and was still bad. After half a year, however, he changed quite a bit. This change is not simply a matter of a change in behavior; it also enables others to sense the presence of the Lord and to feel that there is the taste of the Lord in him.

Some people may be very meek, but there is no taste of the Lord within them. Yet with others, there is the taste of the Lord in their meekness. Why is this? It is because the meekness of some people does not come from inside, it is like something that has been painted on them outwardly or an outward decoration. The meekness of others, however, comes from the permeation of the Lord's life within them. These ones not only have meekness, but they also have the Lord in their meekness. In fact, we can say that their meekness is just the Lord Himself.

For example, suppose there are two brothers. By nature the older one honors his parents, but by nature the younger is disobedient to his parents. One day the younger one gets saved, and the Spirit of the Lord and the life of the Lord entered into his spirit. At this time, outwardly, the younger one is not as good at honoring his parents as the older brother. However, although the older brother is good at honoring his parents, God's Spirit and God's life are not inside of him. Thus, from the beginning of the year to the end of the year, the older brother honors his parents in his natural way. When the young brother got saved in the summer, his outward behavior at that time was not as good as his older brother's. However, at the end of the year, after six months, the younger brother also honors his parents. Yet how does he honor his parents? He honors his parents by the Lord's Spirit and life that have permeated him. The Lord's Spirit and life permeate his disobedient nature and begin to work on his disobedience. Eventually, his disobeying becomes honoring. Thus, by the end of the year, both of them honor their parents.

At this time, the older brother's honoring is just his natural honoring, but the younger brother's honoring is different. When others touch the younger brother's honoring, they not only touch his honoring, they also touch the Lord. There is the taste of the Lord in his honoring. The difference between these two kinds of honoring is that the older brother's honoring is of his natural man—it is human behavior—and the younger brother's honoring comes from the inward permeation of the Lord—it is the Lord's life living out from him. Both honor their parents, but their honoring has two different natures and tastes. One is merely behavior, but the other is life. One has the taste of man, whereas the other has the taste of the Lord. This kind of virtue, which comes as a result of being permeated with the Lord's life and the Lord's Spirit, is the expression of the maturity in life, which takes place step by step. This kind of growth and maturity in life is the result of the permeation of the Lord's Spirit and the Lord's life. This permeation begins from our innermost center, our spirit, and continues outwardly into our soul.

HAVING THE LORD'S SPIRIT IN OUR SPIRIT THROUGH SALVATION, BUT STILL NOT HAVING THE LORD'S SPIRIT IN OUR SOUL

Our soul has three parts—our mind, emotion, and will. These three components represent our whole being. Looking from the outside, our whole person is comprised of the activities of these three parts—the mind, emotion, and will. Our thinking, consideration, and reasoning are functions of the mind. Our likes, dislikes, and feelings of joy, anger, sorrow, and delight are the functions of the emotion. To decide, determine, and choose are functions of the will. Our living cannot be separated from these three parts. When we were saved, the Lord's life and the Lord's Spirit entered into our spirit. However, our mind, emotion, and will still may not have the Spirit of the Lord. When we think, consider, and reason, the Lord may not be in our thoughts, considerations, and reasonings. Of course, when we pray, we are in spirit, we have fellowship with the Lord, we feel the presence of the Lord, and we can touch the Lord. But as soon as we finish our prayer, our mind begins to think about our business, our studies, or our children. The Spirit is not in our mind at all.

When we first get saved, the Spirit is not only not in our mind, the Spirit is also not in our emotion. For example, we may have morning watch in our room in the morning. In our morning watch we may touch the Lord's presence in our spirit. This experience may be very sweet and joyful. However, when we come out from our room, we may find one of our family members doing something improper. As a result, our emotion is stirred up, and we lose our temper immediately. In the morning when we pray in our room, we touch the Lord and are in our spirit. However, right after we finish praying, our emotion is stirred up, and we become joyful or angry, sorrowful or delighted. From this we see that there is no Spirit in our emotion. The will is also the same. When we pray, we have enjoyment in our spirit. However, after we finish praying, our ideas and choices immediately come out, and no one can change them. This indicates that the Spirit is not in our will. Therefore, we see that as a result of our salvation we have the Lord's Spirit and the Lord's life in our spirit, but we may not yet have the Spirit in our mind, emotion, and will. At the time of our salvation, our whole outer being still has no Spirit. Thus, when people touch us, they may not sense that we are sinful or that we are doing something wrong, but they also may not sense that we have God or the taste of the Lord. Although we have been saved and have the Lord's Spirit and the Lord's life in our spirit, the Lord's Spirit may not yet have permeated and expanded into our mind, emotion, and will.

A MATURE CHRISTIAN BEING ONE
WHOSE SPIRIT AND SOUL ARE FILLED
WITH THE LORD AND THE SPIRIT

If a Christian has the proper growth in life, when you touch his thoughts, you will sense the taste of the Lord in it; when you touch his likes or even his dislikes, you will sense the taste of the Lord; and if you watch the way he decides and chooses, you will also sense the taste of the Lord. Why is this? It is because he allows the Lord's Spirit and the Lord's life to permeate from his spirit into his mind, emotion, and will. That is, he allows the Lord's life to spread and expand in him and also allows the Lord's life in him to grow step by step and to mature little by little. In the same way, the more the fruit on a tree grows, the more it matures. One day the Lord's Spirit and life will permeate our whole being completely, causing our whole being to be filled with the Lord and to have the taste of the Lord in full. When this happens, we will be mature believers. Not only will we be blameless in our daily walk, but when others touch us, they will be able to sense the taste of the Lord in our thoughts, preferences, and ideas. This will be the case because the Lord's Spirit and life will have spread from our spirit to every part of our soul.

THE HEART OF A MAN REPRESENTING HIS PERSON

Here we would like to elaborate on a particular matter—our heart. The spirit of man is the deepest and most central part of his whole being. Man's soul is his outer man. The soul includes the mind, emotion, and will. Man's heart also includes many things. Man's heart has thoughts, desires, and intentions (Heb. 4:12). Thus, our heart includes our mind, emotion, and will—the three parts of the soul. Thus, our mind, emotion, and will are all a matter of the heart.

Hebrews 10:22 also reveals that our conscience is in our heart. The heart includes the conscience, and the conscience is part of the spirit. The spirit also has three parts—intuition, fellowship, and conscience. In summary, the heart is the mind, emotion, and will plus the conscience. The conscience is in our spirit, our deepest part, and surrounding our conscience is our mind, emotion, and will. Thus, our heart has four parts— first, the conscience; second, the mind; third, the emotion; and fourth, the will. Among these four parts—conscience, mind, emotion, and will—one part is in the spirit and three parts are in the soul. Thus, the heart is connected to the spirit as well as to the soul. In other words, the heart is where our spirit and our soul converge. The heart is the converging place of our being. Therefore, the heart represents a person. When we believe that a person is bad, we often say that his heart is bad. In addition, when the heart is absent, the person is absent. Sometimes, a person is present, but his heart is absent. In such a case, the person might as well be absent since only the heart can represent a person.

THE HEART BEING THE GATEWAY

Those who study the Bible all agree that God's Spirit and God's life being in our spirit means that they are in the intuition and fellowship of our spirit, our most central part. But the spirit of man not only has the intuition and the fellowship; it also has the conscience. Hence, God's Spirit and life, which are in our spirit, also touch our heart. When God's Spirit and life spread from our spirit, they go through our heart. Therefore, our heart is the key, the gateway. Whether God's Spirit and life within us can spread to our mind, emotion, and will depends upon whether our heart allows God to pass through it.

When a person is saved, God enters into him and becomes one with him. Before a person is saved, he lives in his mind, emotion, will, and conscience. This is where he is. Once he is saved, God enters into him. Which part of him is God in? God is in his spirit. Thus, there is something between God and man. This something is the heart. Thus, everything depends upon whether our heart is turned to the Lord or away from the Lord. When our heart is turned away from the Lord, then we are turned away from the Lord. When our heart is turned to the Lord, we are turned to the Lord. Second Corinthians 3:16 says, "But whenever their heart turns to the Lord, the veil is taken away." Why is it that whenever the heart turns to the Lord, the veil is removed? The reason is that man's turned away heart is the veil. If a person has his back toward us, he cannot see us. That is the veil. When the heart is turned to the Lord, man is face to face with the Lord, and naturally, the veil is taken away.

Even though many of us are saved and have the Lord in our spirit, our heart often separates us from the Lord. In a sense, the Lord is on the inside, we are on the outside, and the heart is between us, so that we and the Lord cannot be face to face. Thus, everything depends upon where our heart is facing. When our heart is toward the Lord, there are no problems. We and the Lord are face to face. But when our heart is turned away from the Lord, then we are turned away from the Lord, and spontaneously, there is no communication with the Lord. So, the heart is an important gateway.

THE LORD BEING THE SPIRIT, AND WHERE THE SPIRIT OF THE LORD IS, THERE BEING FREEDOM

Second Corinthians 3:17 says, "And the Lord is the Spirit; and where the Spirit of the Lord is, there is freedom." Our heart needs to turn to the Lord, and the Lord is the Spirit. Thus, our heart must turn to the Spirit. The Spirit is within us today. We have to turn to the Lord, the Spirit, within us. This is wonderful. We have to learn to turn within to our spirit to fellowship with the Lord so that we can be mingled with the Spirit. We are always facing the outside and are turned away from the Lord. Thus, we have to learn to turn within where the Lord is. The Lord is the Spirit, so when we turn to the Lord we are turning to the Spirit. In addition, the Spirit is within us. Thus, in order to turn to the Lord, we have to turn to our spirit within. When we turn back to our spirit within, we sense the presence of the Lord. However, whenever we turn to the outside, to the soul, there is no presence of the Lord.

The Lord is the Spirit within us, our person is on the outside, and our heart is in between the Lord and us. When the heart turns outward, it turns away from the Lord. This is the veil. When the heart turns inward, it turns to the Lord, and the veil is taken away. How do we know if we are turning to the Lord or turning away from the Lord? In 2 Corinthians 3 Paul says the Lord is the Spirit and that where the Spirit of the Lord is, there is freedom. Freedom is the big proof. Where the Lord is, there is freedom. When the Lord is in our mind, our mind is freed. When the Lord is in our emotion, our emotion is freed. And when Lord is in our will, our will is freed.

Many people testify that after they are saved, as long as they do not sin, their life is quite peaceful. But after they hear about turning to the spirit within, their life is no longer as peaceful and as free. They cannot buy clothes, go to the movies, or go to dancing parties as they wish. Now there seems to be many limitations. In the past they could do whatever they wanted to do. As long as they did not sin, did not hurt anyone, and went to the meeting on the Lord's Day, they seemed to have peace within. But now, there is no peace. When they turn to their deepest part, to the spirit, they cannot do this or do that.

Some young Christians complain, saying, "The elderly saints saw many movies and enjoyed life to the full when they were young, and now they speak to us about spirituality. However, we have not seen enough movies and have not enjoyed life enough. We do not want to lose our freedom so early. Can we not wait until we are fifty years old before we start to love the Lord?" We must realize that we can dance, but we will not have freedom in our mind. We can watch movies, but we will not have freedom in our emotion. We can choose to drink, but we will not have freedom in our will. Our entire being is completely restricted and bound and has no freedom. A person who loves the Lord and allows the Spirit to pass through him may not seem to have any freedom outwardly—he cannot go to the movie theater, attend parties, or dance. But within him there is freedom—his mind is freed, his emotion is freed, and his will is freed. Moreover, his conscience is also freed.

No Christian has freedom in his conscience when he is at a dancing party. No Christian has peace in his conscience when he is in a movie theater. His conscience accuses and condemns him because his heart is turned away from the Lord. However, whenever his heart turns to the Lord, the Lord as the Spirit enters into him, and when the Spirit enters, freedom also enters. The Spirit is freedom. When you dance, enjoy life, go shopping in shopping centers, do you have freedom in your spirit? Do you have freedom in your emotion? Do you have freedom in your will? Do you have freedom in your mind? You yourself know that this is a painful experience. An unbeliever can dance as much as he likes and still be happy. But if you have been saved, not only do you not have peace within when you are dancing, but you feel bad even after you go home. Your conscience condemns you, your emotion is not at peace, your will is not at ease, and your mind is bothered. This is a painful experience. This is the situation of a Christian who loves the world.

If a Christian loves the world, his heart cannot love the Lord. The heart comprises the conscience, mind, emotion, and will. A Christian who loves the world and does not love the Lord does not have peace in any of these parts. He has no freedom within. However, whenever his heart turns to the Lord and says to Him, "Lord, I love You. Even though movies are lovable, I love You. Even though dancing is lovable, I love You. Even though entertainment, friends, and fashion are all lovable, I love You and my heart turns to You." Then the veil within him is removed, he touches the Spirit, and wherever the Lord is, there is freedom. His mind follows him to love the Lord, so his mind has freedom. His emotion follows him to love the Lord, so his emotion has freedom. His will follows him to love the Lord—his decisions are according to the Lord's decisions, and his opinions are according to the Lord's opinions—so his will also has freedom.

If this is not the case, his mind, emotion, and will are under bondage, and his conscience condemns him. But when his mind thinks about the Lord, his emotion loves the Lord, and his will chooses the Lord, his conscience will approve of him. The center of his whole being is at ease and free. At this time the freedom that he experiences is real freedom—an inward freedom, a freedom full of joy and peace. Then God's glory and image will be lived out of this person.

CHAPTER TWELVE

THE WAY FOR A CHRISTIAN
TO MATURE IN LIFE—FROM HAVING THE LORD
TO HAVING THE LORD'S IMAGE

FIVE IMPORTANT MATTERS

Second Corinthians 3:17-18 says, "And the Lord is the Spirit; and where the Spirit of the Lord is, there is freedom. But we all with unveiled face, beholding and reflecting like a mirror the glory of the Lord, are being transformed into the same image from glory to glory, even as from the Lord Spirit." In these two verses, there are five important matters. The first is the Lord, the second is the Spirit, the third is freedom, the fourth is glory, and the fifth is image.

Verse 17, which says, "And the Lord is the Spirit; and where the Spirit of the Lord is, there is freedom," joins three of these matters together—the Lord, the Spirit, and freedom. Verse 18 then says, "But we all with unveiled face, behold-ing...the glory of the Lord, are being transformed into the same image from glory to glory." This shows us that when we behold the glory of the Lord, we are transformed into His image from glory to glory, even as from the Lord Spirit. This verse joins all five matters together. At the beginning of verse 17, there is the Lord Himself; at the end of verse 18, there is the image of the Lord; and in between these two matters are three others—the Spirit, freedom, and glory. To go from the first item to the last—from the Lord to the image of the Lord—we need to pass through the Spirit, freedom, and glory.

THE HEART BEING THE GATEWAY
FOR THE SPIRIT TO ENTER INTO THE SOUL

Maturity in the Christian life is to go from having the

Lord to having the Lord's image. In other words, to go from having only the Lord to having the Lord's image as well is the way for a Christian to mature in life. The Lord is the Spirit, and when we were saved, He entered into our spirit. Our spirit is the center of our being. Around this center are the different parts of our soul. Originally, we did not have the Spirit of the Lord, the Lord Himself, in our being—neither in our spirit nor in our soul. We also did not have the elements of the Lord. Therefore, we did not have the form of the Lord or the image of the Lord. When we got saved, God regenerated us, and the Spirit of the Lord entered into our spirit. From then on, this Lord Spirit has been in our spirit and has been trying to spread from our spirit to our soul. In order for Him to do this, He has to pass through a gateway. This gateway is our heart. The heart is a gateway between our spirit and our soul, joining the spirit to the soul. If the heart does not open the gate and allow the spirit to be released, the Spirit has no way to get into the soul. Therefore, 2 Corinthians 3:16 speaks of the importance of the heart. It says, "Whenever their heart turns to the Lord, the veil is taken away." The veil is taken away because the heart turns to the Lord. This means that in order for us to be face to face with the Lord, our heart must turn to the Lord.

Although we have been saved, instead of being toward the Lord, our heart is often toward many things other than the Lord. Because our heart turns away from the Lord, there is a veil between the Lord and us. We cannot see Him, and we are not able to fellowship with Him face to face. This is the situation until the day that our heart turns to Him, and the veil is taken away. Then we see Him and are face to face with Him. This shows us that the heart is the key. The fact that the heart is between the spirit and the soul means that the heart is between man and the Lord. If a man's heart is toward the Lord, he is face to face with the Lord, and he can fellowship with the Lord directly. However, if his heart is toward things other than the Lord and is turned away from the Lord, there will be a veil, a barrier, between the Lord and him. If a person closes his heart to the Lord, he locks the Lord in his spirit. If the heart is turned away from the Lord, the Lord is detained and held in the spirit.

THE REASON FOR IMMATURITY
IN THE CHRISTIAN LIFE—
THE LORD HAVING NO GROUND

If someone were to ask us whether or not we are saved, surely we would say that we are. If someone were also to ask us whether or not the Lord is within us, we certainly would say that He is. However, if someone were to ask us whether or not the Lord has spread out from our spirit, we may not have anything to say. The reason is that our heart is often closed toward the Lord, and the Lord is detained in our spirit to the extent that He cannot come out. Although the Lord is within us, it is as if He is surrounded by signs that say, "No Thoroughfare." Thus, the Lord is not able to move within us even a little bit, and He does not have any chance to come out of us. We have the Lord in our spirit, but we do not have the Lord in the different parts of our soul; that is, we do not have the Lord in our mind, emotion, and will.

We have been saved, and the Lord is within us, but the Lord cannot come out of us. This does not mean that we do not acknowledge the Lord at all; it means that there is no ground for the Lord in our thoughts. We think about this and that, but we do not think about the Lord. There is also no ground for the Lord in our emotions. We love many things, but we do not love the Lord. Moreover, there is no ground for the Lord in our will—in our decisions and choices. Our self has all the ground. Although we have been saved and have the Lord in our spirit, the Lord cannot come out from our spirit to control our mind, emotion, and will. We believe in the Lord and have the Lord, but our mind, emotion, and will are independent of the Lord, and the Lord has no ground in these three parts of our soul. This is the reason why we are not mature in life.

TURNING THE HEART TO THE LORD
BEING THE KEY TO GROWING IN LIFE

We are not able to mature in the Lord's life because the Lord's Spirit and life are not able to grow out from within our spirit. The reason for this is that our heart is often closed to the Lord. In order for us to grow in life, our heart must be open to the Lord, and our mind, emotion, and will must be opened to the Lord. Once these three parts are open, the Lord will be able to spread out from our spirit into our mind, emotion, and will to reach these different parts of our soul.

How do we open our heart to the Lord? Whenever we have to make a determination or decision, we should first say to the Lord, "O Lord, I love You. I am willing to please You." This kind of prayer opens our will to the Lord, and once our will is opened, the Lord will enter into it. In addition, whenever we love or desire something, we should stop for a moment and say to the Lord, "O Lord, I love You. I want to please You." This opens our emotion to the Lord. When we do this, the Lord will surely enter into our emotion. Similarly, whenever we begin to think about something, we should stop our thinking for a moment and say to the Lord, "O Lord, I love You. I want to please You." This kind of statement opens our mind to the Lord, and through this opening, the Lord will be able to enter into our mind.

Whenever we open to the Lord in our mind, the Lord's Spirit will gain the opportunity to enter into the different parts of our soul. Some saints say that it is not easy to touch the Spirit. This is true; it not easy to touch the Spirit. Yet the Spirit is able to be sensed. In other words, the Spirit produces feelings within us. These feelings are a manifestation of the Spirit. We can liken this to electricity. We cannot touch electricity, but we can see light, which is a manifestation of electricity. Similarly, the Spirit is in us, and although we cannot touch the Spirit, we can sense Him. When we sit next to a fan, we can feel the result of the functioning of electricity. In like manner, we can feel the result of the functioning of the Spirit.

PAYING ATTENTION TO
THE SENSE OF THE SPIRIT IN US

What is the sense of the Spirit in us? We can illustrate this with the following example. One day you may want to visit one of the saints, so you do so. However, in the deepest part of your being, there is a sense. This sense is entirely different from your own thinking. In your thinking you want to go visit this saint, but your sense within does not agree. This sense comes from the Spirit who is within you. Christians are very special because they have the Spirit of God abiding within them. Many times when we have a certain determination in our mind, emotion, and will, we simply have another feeling within us. This feeling is in our deepest part and comes from the function of our spirit. The Spirit of the Lord abides in our spirit and has been mingled with our spirit to become one spirit (1 Cor. 6:17).

Whenever our heart opens to the Lord, this Spirit spreads out from within us into our mind, emotion, and will. How do we know the Lord's Spirit has spread into our mind, emotion, and will? There is one obvious proof. This proof is the freedom mentioned in 2 Corinthians 3:17—"And the Lord is the Spirit; and where the Spirit of the Lord is, there is freedom." Once you have the Spirit of the Lord in your mind, your mind will have freedom. Once you have the Spirit of the Lord in your emotion, your emotion will also have freedom. And once you have the Spirit of the Lord in your will, it will surely be freed.

What is it actually like to have freedom in one's mind, emotion, and will? Suppose that a sister goes to buy some clothing, sees some fashionable and fancy clothes, and wants to buy them. However, at that very moment, there is a feeling in her deepest part. She feels that it is unsuitable for someone who loves the Lord to wear fashionable and fancy clothing of this kind. This is the Lord's feeling within her. The critical question in this situation is, which direction is this sister's heart facing? If her heart is toward the fancy clothes, it will spontaneously be closed to the Lord. If this is the case, the Lord's Spirit will not be able to enter into her mind, emotion, and will, and she will not have any freedom within her. If, however, her heart is toward the Lord, she will forsake the clothing. Then the Lord's Spirit will have the opportunity to enter into her mind, emotion, and will, and she will have freedom within her.

Many sisters have this kind of experience. If their hearts are toward the clothes and they buy them, they will be unable to pray for three days. Then since they are unable to pray for three days, they will become low. They will not be released and will not be able to stand. This is what it means to not have freedom. When people meet these sisters, they will think that there is something wrong with them. These sister's countenances will be miserable and they will appear to be bound by something. Even in their speaking, they will sound unnatural and restrained. In the meetings they will not be able to pray to the extent that they will not even be able to say "amen" when others pray. This is because they are bound and do not have any freedom. We must remember that whenever the Lord's Spirit is bound within us, we are surely restrained. Many Christians are not joyful because the Spirit within them is not joyful. When the Spirit within them is joyful, then they will be joyful.

If the sisters love the Lord, face the Lord, and say to Him, "O Lord, I love You. I want to please You. I do not want these clothes. I will not buy them," then immediately they will be released and will have freedom within them. Then they will be able to pray, sing hymns, and say "hallelujah." In the meeting, they certainly will be released. When people meet them, they will meet a spirit that is uplifted and soaring with joy. They will sense the taste of the Lord with them. If someone says that a meeting is boring, we must realize that it is he himself who is bored within. Because his spirit, his inner being, is bored, he feels that everything is boring. This is not only the case for spiritual things but also for ordinary things. When a man comes across something joyful, his heart will be filled with joy. Then when he meets people on the way, he will feel that they are lovely, and when he lifts up his head to see the clouds, he will find them pleasant. To the contrary, if he comes across something sad, he will be filled with sadness and sorrow. Then even if he meets the same people, the same earth, the same sky, and the same clouds, he will feel sad.

WHERE THE SPIRIT OF THE LORD IS, THERE BEING FREEDOM

Why is it that the same situation can lead to two kinds of feelings? It is because we can have two moods. We can feel bored or released in response to the same meeting. Thus, the self is present in both the feeling of boredom and that of release. If you are depressed inside, you will feel that the meeting is low. If you are released, you will feel that the meeting is released. Where is the source of this state of being released or depressed? It is within you, and it depends on whether or not the Spirit of the Lord is free or restrained. If you do not let the Spirit of the Lord spread out of you, you will be restrained and depressed. Once this bondage is within you, your mind, emotion, and will are not at ease. Your mind, emotion, and will are not released and thus have no joy. The Lord is the Spirit, and the Spirit Himself is freedom. Thus, if you do not let the Spirit pass through you, surely you will not have freedom.

We all know that wherever there is a wind, it is cool. The wind brings in coolness. If several of us are sitting in a house, and if all the windows and doors are shut and the fan is broken, it will be very stuffy. However, if we open the doors and windows and repair the fan, then there will be a wind, and we will feel cool while sitting in the house. Coolness comes from the wind, and wherever there is a wind, it is cool. Thus, we can say that the wind is the coolness. Similarly, where the Spirit of the Lord is, there is freedom. The Spirit of the Lord is the freedom. Thus, if you do not let the Spirit of the Lord have the ground in your mind, emotion, and will, one thing is certain—your mind, emotion, and will shall all be depressed. Christians who love to go to the movies and to go dancing may feel very comfortable when they see a movie or when they go to a dance. But when they get home afterward, the boredom and depression within them will deepen. Sometimes this feeling of boredom and depression will last for a few days.

For every Christian who loves the world, the more they love the world, the more they are bored within. For those who live according to themselves, the more they live this way, the more they are depressed within. Spiritual things are very real, and no one can cheat. The Holy Spirit in us has His own law, and this law is very real. If we love the Lord more and allow the Lord to overcome more in us, we will be released, free, and clear inside. Although there may be persecution or difficult environments outwardly, our mind, emotion, and will certainly will be open and free. This is because the Spirit is within us, and wherever the Spirit is, there is freedom. The Lord as the Spirit is the freedom. The three—the Lord, the Spirit, and freedom—are actually one.

THE SECRET TO EXPERIENCING FREEDOM IN THE SPIRIT— HAVING OUR HEART OPEN TO THE LORD

The Lord is in us, and if we let Him move freely in us and obey Him more, He will have the ground and will expand in us. The Spirit of the Lord will also be able to operate, for the Lord is the Spirit. Once that Spirit operates, moves, and enters into our mind, our mind is free. When He enters into our emotion, our emotion is released. When He enters into our entire being, our entire being is released and free. For an example, there is a saint in the church life who is fresh and living. Twenty years ago he was fresh and living, and twenty years later he is still fresh and living. When you see him in Shanghai, he is fresh and living. When you see him in Hong Kong, he is fresh and living. And when you see him in Taiwan, he is still fresh and living. It seems that he has never been depressed. His secret is that his spirit is free and fresh. Once there is even a small amount of bondage in his spirit, he kneels down and prays to the Lord. He asks the Lord for forgiveness and the cleansing of His blood. His heart is always toward the Lord. Therefore, his spirit is free. Once his spirit is free, he is free—his mind, emotion, and will are all free.

Is this kind of person free from having any burdens, difficulties, or pain? If we were to ask him, he would tell us that his burdens, difficulties, and pain are by no means lighter than ours. The difference is that he always allows the Spirit to be free and endeavors to always keep his heart toward the Lord. Every time that a burden or a difficulty comes, he simply turns to the Lord and says to Him, "O Lord, I give this to You." Satan does not stop working, so burdens and difficulties still come to him one after another, but he keeps turning to the Lord and saying to Him, "O Lord, I give this to You." Again and again, he allows the Spirit to be free in this way. We should never say that we can sing praises to the Lord only when we do not have any difficulty or burden. Freedom depends upon the Spirit's being able to spread out of us. The Spirit is in us, and in order for Him to spread out of us, our heart must be open. We should not be afraid of burdens and difficulties. When the burdens and difficulties come, we must turn our heart to the Lord. Regardless of what the environments may be, what troublesome matters there are, what the desires of our heart are, what decisions or determinations there are to be made, our heart must be open to the Lord. This is the secret.

In John 3:8, the Holy Spirit is likened to the wind, and everyone who is born of the Spirit is likened to the blowing wind. Once we open the windows, the wind comes into the house and fills it. Similarly, once our heart opens, the Spirit comes out and enters into our mind, emotion, and will. The Spirit is freedom, and where the Spirit is, there is freedom. Once the Spirit gets into our mind, emotion, and will, we are released, transcendent, and free. Outwardly the environment does not change, and we still have difficulties upon us. Yet our heart within us is full of freedom. There are many burdens upon us, yet our heart is released. This freedom, this release, is the Spirit. We all have had this kind of experience. We have difficulties, burdens, problems, and pains, yet whenever our heart turns to the Lord, the Spirit within us comes out and enters into our emotion, mind, and will, causing our entire being to be free and released.

WHEREVER THERE IS FREEDOM, THERE BEING GLORY

Whenever our heart turns to the Lord, the veil is taken away. Then we with unveiled face are able to meet the Lord face to face and behold His glory. The Lord is the Spirit, the Spirit is freedom, and freedom is glory, which is God expressed. How do we know that we are experiencing glory? It is the same as freedom. Whenever we feel released, comfortable, and easy, that is freedom. Whenever we feel noble, honorable, and transcendent, that is glory. When the saints are going to a movie, they have a feeling within them that they should not go. However, some of them struggle within, do not obey, and still go. Then when they arrive at the theater, they have no peace, so they look around to see if there are any other brothers or sisters there. Then they quickly go into the theater. When they go home after the movie, they feel that they are so low and cannot stand upright. When they come to the meeting, they surely will not lift up their heads. Their spirits will not be able to rise up. What kind of feeling is this? Is this glory? It is not. In fact, this kind of feeling is the opposite of glory.

Suppose you want to go to the movies, but because you do not have peace within, you say to the Lord, "O Lord, I love You. I want to please You." Then after saying this, you do not go. As a result, you will be a transcendent Christian, and when you go to the meeting, you will be soaring inside. This is not pride; it is a bright, shining, and transcendent feeling that comes from having the presence of the Lord and the beauty and joy of the Lord. This is glory. Such an experience cannot be described. It is clear, shining, and glorious, and it causes you to feel comfortable. This is the experience of glory. Where the Spirit is, there is freedom, and where there is freedom, there is glory.

Even if he does not go to the movies, if a normal Christian loses his temper a little at home, when he sees the saints, he will feel cowardly and will be afraid of seeing their faces. Why is this? It is because he feels low and lacking within. He is not released. However, if he overcomes at home and allows the Lord to have the ground, when he sees a saint in the distance, he will immediately catch up with him and greet him. In addition, others will see that his face is shining just like Moses' face shone with glory. Such a condition is the result of seeing the glory of the Lord face to face.

BEING TRANSFORMED
INTO THE IMAGE OF THE LORD
FROM GLORY TO GLORY

Second Corinthians 3:18 also includes the phrase *reflecting like a mirror*. If we have our face covered with a veil, there will be a barrier between the light and us. It is not until we have the veil taken away that our face and the light can be face to face. Then we can see the light. This is like the reflecting of a mirror. Because the Spirit is in us, we have freedom, our face is unveiled to the Lord, and we are face to face with Him. His glory shines upon our face, and we reflect His glory like a mirror. We cannot pretend to do this. Only when we meet a brother who has God's shining and glory on his face, will we immediately feel God's presence and sense that God is being expressed.

Many times when we meet one of the saints, we groan within and are sad. Although this one is a believer, he seems to have fallen down to the ground. He is unable to get up and cannot move. On the other hand, sometimes when we meet one of the saints, we bow down and worship the Lord, realizing that this is a man who is ascendant and standing upright. He is a man who is standing on the ground and reaching to the heavens. He is active and is able to fight. We sense that this man has glory—the glory of God is on his face. This is glory. Where does this glory come from? It comes from having freedom. What is freedom? Freedom is the Spirit. And who is the Spirit? The Spirit is the Lord. The four—the Lord, the Spirit, freedom, and glory—are actually one.

When our heart turns to the Lord, the veil is taken away. Then our entire being is set free, and we reflect like a mirror. Eventually, we see the glory of the Lord, and from this glory to the ultimate glory, we are being transformed into the image of the Lord. This very image is glory. People will be able to see the Lord, the image of the Lord, in us. Where does this image come from? It comes from glory, and this glory comes from freedom, freedom comes from the Spirit, and the Spirit is the Lord Himself. Where is this Spirit? This Spirit is in our spirit. The Lord is the Spirit, and He is in our spirit. When our heart loves Him and opens to Him, He comes out. And when He comes out, when He moves, He is the Spirit. Whenever the Lord moves and acts, He is the Spirit; and whenever the Spirit comes out and enters into our mind, emotion, and will, He is freedom. Then the Spirit of the Lord is in our entire being, and our entire being is set free. This freedom is glory, which is the presence of God and the expression of God. This makes us feel noble, honorable, and glorious. This is glory, and this is the image of the Lord.

If day by day we love the Lord and give Him the opportunities, day by day the Lord will spread out from within us. Then we will grow and be transformed day by day. Ultimately we will be transformed into the image of the Lord. Originally we had only the Lord within us, but through transformation we will have the image of the Lord within us. This image is the Lord Himself. People will realize that we have a certain condition. This condition is the image of the Lord. We can also call this a condition of having glory, freedom, release, the presence of the Lord, and the Lord's Spirit. These five things are actually one. The Lord is the Spirit, and where the Spirit of the Lord is, there is freedom. When we have freedom, our face is unveiled to see the glory of the Lord. Then, from glory to glory, we are transformed into the image of the Lord.

When the Lord lives out from within us, we grow and become mature. Therefore, we need to open our heart to the Lord and let Him spread out from our spirit into our mind, emotion, and will. Once He enters into these parts of us, we are free, we have glory, and we are honorable. At this time we have His image. When our mind is like His mind, our desires are like His desires, and our decisions are like His decisions, we will have His image.

CHAPTER THIRTEEN

THE WAY FOR A CHRISTIAN TO MATURE IN LIFE— WALKING ACCORDING TO THE SPIRIT

Second Corinthians 3:17-18 mentions five important matters—the Lord, the Spirit, freedom, glory, and image. After the Lord resurrected and ascended, He became the life-giving Spirit (1 Cor. 15:45). The Lord Jesus' incarnation was His becoming flesh; His death and resurrection were His becoming the Spirit. Christians always speak of loving the Lord, worshiping the Lord, obeying the Lord, and following the Lord, but where is the Lord? Second Corinthians 3 shows us that the Lord is the Spirit and indicates that the Lord is in our spirit. Even before the Lord's death and resurrection, John 4:24 tells us that God is Spirit and that if man wants to worship Him, he must worship Him neither in Jerusalem nor Samaria but in his spirit.

THE LORD BEING THE SPIRIT IN OUR SPIRIT

What is the Lord? The Lord is the Spirit. Where is the Lord? The Lord is in our spirit. We may have the concept that the Lord is in heaven. Truly, the Lord is the Lord of heaven, but He is also the Spirit in our spirit. The Lord is wherever the Spirit is, and the way the Lord contacts man is in man's spirit. We can use electricity as an illustration. Electricity is essential for our daily living. On the one hand, electricity is in the air; on the other hand, it is in our room and we are able to contact it. Our unbelieving friends often ask, "Where is God? Where is the Lord? Can He be seen or touched?" Those who have experienced this know that God is Spirit, that the Lord is the Spirit, and that the Lord is in our spirit today. He is not only very near to us; He is even mingled with us as one. No matter where we are, by the Lord's precious blood and in His name, we can touch Him as the Spirit.

When we believe into the Lord, we believe into the Lord who is in heaven. At that time, we open our heart and our spirit to Him. Then we sense His presence in our spirit, in the depths of our being. This is the testimony of everyone who has been saved. As we open our heart and spirit to the Lord who is in heaven, we feel peaceful, proper, enlightened, comfortable, strengthened, and satisfied within. Every genuine believer can testify that although they believed into the Lord who is in heaven, at the moment they believed, the Lord entered into them. Moreover, they can testify that from the time that they first believed, many times throughout their Christian life they have sensed the Lord in heaven touch their inner being and cause them to feel peaceful and secure within.

THE CHRISTIAN LIFE BEING
TO HAVE THE LORD AS EVERYTHING WITHIN

The fact that we can sense the Lord within us shows us that the Lord is the Spirit and that He contacts us in our spirit. After we are saved, everything of the spiritual life comes from the Lord's moving within us. Even now when I am speaking here, apparently I am the one speaking, but actually there is One who is speaking within me as my content, filling me and sustaining me to speak. Otherwise, how could it be that the more I speak, the more I have to speak, and the more I speak, the more I have the Lord's presence? If I speak from myself, then after I have given three to five messages, I will have nothing more to say. It is the same with the teachings concerning the Christian life. Some say that these teachings are too high and that they are too difficult to follow. They say, "Not only do we need to love our enemies, but as Matthew 5:39 says, we also need to turn our left cheek to those who slap us on our right cheek. Who is able to do this?" We must realize that no Christian is able to do this by himself but by the Lord who dwells within. He takes every opportunity to fill us, replace us, and work within us to enable us to live this way.

Consider, for example, the motion of an electric fan. It rotates quickly and smoothly. From the outside, it appears as if the electric fan is rotating by itself, but in actuality there is a motor within the fan that pushes the fan and causes it to rotate. The living of a genuine Christian is like this—it comes from the Lord's "pushing" within. Andrew Murray was a brother who knew the spiritual life. He once asked, "What is prayer?" He then said that prayer is the Christ who is indwelling us praying to the Christ who is sitting on the throne. This word is very clear and to the point. Genuine prayer involves not only the person who is praying but also the Lord who dwells within him. The Lord "puts us on" and prays from within us. If we are covered by some clothing, when we move around, although others may see the clothing moving, the fact is that we are the ones who are moving within the clothing.

The Christian life is the Lord putting us on and living out from within us. Proper prayer is not simply us praying but is the Spirit in us putting us on to pray. The Spirit is the Lord Himself. Romans 8 says that although we do not know how to pray, the Spirit within us prays for us (v. 26). Similarly, we do not know how to love people or how to obey our parents. Even if we do know how to do these things a little bit, our ability is very limited. When our parents lose their temper, we are unhappy with them, but when our parents are pleased with us, we honor them. This kind of honoring is not from the Lord within. What the Lord does from within us does not depend upon how our parents treat us. The Lord would still honor them from within us regardless of how they treat us. This is something that we cannot do from ourselves. We can do it only by the Spirit motivating us from within.

THE SPIRIT BEING OUR UNLIMITED STRENGTH

We were all created by the Lord with some good elements. Thus, by ourselves we can do good things. However, our goodness is very limited and natural. Our patience, meekness, humility, goodness, and forgiveness are all limited. On the contrary, what is motivated from within us by the Spirit is unlimited. The good that we do from ourselves can be likened to using our strength to rotate the blades of an electric fan.

We can cause the fan to rotate for a while, but it will stop immediately afterward. However, if electricity is transmitted to the fan, once it is switched on, the electric fan will rotate from morning to evening, even for days without stopping. Similarly, there is no limit to the Lord's motivation in us. This motivation is the Spirit in us as our strength.

FREEDOM BEING WHERE THE SPIRIT OF THE LORD IS

The Spirit of the Lord is the Lord Himself. The Lord today is not only the Lord, but He is also the Spirit. Because He is the Spirit, He can enter into man; because He is the Spirit, He cannot be limited and can be with man all the time. Regardless of the time and place, He is always within us. Second Corinthians 3:17 says that where this Spirit is, there is freedom. The Spirit is in us, but He may not move in us or have the ground in us. Once we allow Him to move in us and have the ground in us, the issue will be freedom. When we have freedom, there is nothing between us and the Lord, and the Lord and we can fellowship with one another.

We have the Spirit in us, and when this Spirit operates and moves within us, we have freedom. We do not have any bondage. This freedom removes all barriers between us and the Lord and allows us to see Him face to face. Then the Lord is expressed and there is glory. Glory is the Lord expressed. When we see the Lord face to face, the Lord appears to us. This is glory. Glory is also the Spirit. The Lord is the Spirit, and the moving of the Spirit is freedom. This freedom enables us to see the Lord, the glory. When we see and experience the Spirit, the result is glory. Moreover, this glory within us is the Lord's image.

FREEDOM, GLORY, AND IMAGE
ALL BEING THE HOLY SPIRIT

In 2 Corinthians 3:17-18 Paul says that where the Spirit of the Lord is, there is freedom. This means that freedom is the Spirit. He also says that when we are free in this way, we can see the glory of the Lord face to face and that when we see the glory of the Lord in this way, we are transformed into the Lord's image from glory to glory. Paul also says that we are transformed from the Lord Spirit. Therefore, this shows us that these five items—freedom, glory, the Lord's image, the Lord, and the Spirit—are all one. The Lord is the Spirit, and the Spirit is freedom, glory, and the Lord's image. The freedom and glory within a Christian and the image expressed from a Christian are all the Holy Spirit Himself.

The freedom within us is the Holy Spirit, the glory expressed from within us is the Holy Spirit, and the image expressed out of us is also the Holy Spirit. This freedom, glory, and image are all the Holy Spirit Himself, and the Holy Spirit is the Lord. The Lord is the Spirit, and the Lord is in our spirit. When this Spirit is in us, we have freedom; when this Spirit is expressed from us, we have glory and the Lord's image. Christians often speak of having the Lord's image and likeness. What is the Lord's image, and what is the Lord's likeness? They are the Spirit. The Spirit is the Lord's likeness, and the Spirit is the Lord's image. Thus, when we live in the Holy Spirit, the Lord's image will be manifested from us.

If a Christian lives by himself all the time and does not live in the Spirit, he will not have freedom, glory, or the Lord's image, because the Spirit will have no ground in him. However, whenever a Christian rejects and denies himself and lives in the Spirit, inwardly he will have freedom. Outwardly he will have glory, and the Lord's image will be manifested from him.

REJECTING THE SELF AND FOLLOWING THE SPIRIT

We need to see that the freedom of a Christian, the glory of a Christian, and the image expressed by a Christian, are all the Holy Spirit Himself. To repeat, the Lord Himself is the Spirit, and when this Spirit lives out of us, the Lord's image is expressed from us. Therefore, to be transformed into the Lord's image means that in every matter in our daily living, whether big or small, we deny ourselves and walk according to the Spirit. In all of our family life, church life, and contact and interaction with others, we must deny and reject our self and live in the Spirit. Then the Lord's image will be expressed from us. If we live in this way every day, rejecting our self and walking according to the Holy Spirit, we will be transformed day by day. Transformation comes when we lay our self down and the Spirit enters into us more and more.

Our self is the flesh, and the Holy Spirit is the Lord Himself. Whenever we live by our self, the flesh is expressed, and whenever we live according to the Holy Spirit, the Lord is expressed. The Lord is the Spirit. This Spirit is the freedom and glory within us and the Lord's image that is expressed out of us. The more we lay our self down and live in the Spirit, the more we will be transformed unto maturity. If we do not live by the self but by the Spirit in every matter—regardless of whether we believe that something is right or wrong, good or bad, and regardless of whether we agree or disagree with it—then we will be transformed. If we do not regard our own views or the views of others and only pay attention to the feeling of the Spirit within us, then we will be those who live according to the Spirit. If we do not trust our own observations or rely on our own thinking but follow the sense in our spirit and care only for that sense, then we will be those who have abandoned the self.

LIVING IN THE SPIRIT AND LETTING THE SPIRIT BE MANIFESTED

As we daily reject our self, care for the sense in our spirit, and walk according to the Spirit, we will be transformed day by day. This transformation will cause us to have the same image as the Lord. The more we have the Lord's image, the more we will become mature, and the more we become mature, the more we will have the Spirit in our soul. Transformation will cause our mind, emotion, and will, that is, our thoughts, preferences, and judgments, to be filled with the Spirit and to have the Lord's image. As a result, our whole being will be filled with the Holy Spirit, and we will become mature. When we become mature, we will be like the prudent virgins in Matthew 25 who not only have oil in their lamps but also have their vessels filled with oil.

Proverbs 20:27 says that the spirit of man is the lamp of Jehovah. Thus, the lamp in Matthew 25 refers to our spirit and the vessel to our person, that is, our soul. When we become mature, not only will we have the Holy Spirit in our spirit, but even our person, our soul, will be full of the Holy Spirit. We will be fully transformed into the Lord's image, we will be mature in life, and we will be ready to be raptured to meet the Lord. In order to reach this stage, we need to reject the self, deny the self, and walk according to the Spirit, putting the self aside in every matter and allowing the Holy Spirit to have the ground. This is to pay the price to buy oil, to prepare oil in our vessels. Only this kind of person—one who lives in the Spirit and allows the Spirit to be expressed—will be made mature and will be raptured to meet the Lord.

CHAPTER FOURTEEN

THE WAY FOR A CHRISTIAN TO MATURE IN LIFE—EXPERIENCING THE WORK OF GOLD, SILVER, AND PRECIOUS STONES

Second Corinthians 3:18 says, "But we all with unveiled face, beholding and reflecting like a mirror the glory of the Lord, are being transformed into the same image from glory to glory, even as from the Lord Spirit." According to this verse we are being transformed into the same image as the Lord by the Lord Spirit. Revelation 4:2b-3a says, "Upon the throne there was One sitting; and He who was sitting was like a jasper stone and a sardius in appearance." It says here that the Lord on the throne was like a jasper stone and a sardius in appearance. Revelation 21:11b says, "Her light was like a most precious stone, like a jasper stone, as clear as crystal." This refers to glory. First Corinthians 3:12 says, "But if anyone builds upon the foundation gold, silver, precious stones, wood, grass, stubble." Gold is first, then silver, and lastly precious stones.

THE TWO ASPECTS OF GOD'S WORK FOR OUR MATURITY IN LIFE

God's work in us is to make us mature in life. God begins His work of making us mature by working His life into us. From then on, God unceasingly works in us so that He can work His life out from within us. When He has worked His life out from within us, we will have reached maturity. When God puts His life into us, He is mingled with us. When He works His life out from within us, we are mingled with Him. When He comes to mingle with us, this is the principle of incarnation. When we mingle with Him in the Holy Spirit, this is the principle of death and resurrection.

THE PRINCIPLES OF INCARNATION AND
DEATH AND RESURRECTION

Every person who has been saved experienced the first aspect of God's work at the time that he was saved. The principle of incarnation is God's entering into us and mingling with us. This is what transpired at the time when we were saved. What God is doing in us now is the second aspect of His work—the principle of death and resurrection. This aspect causes us to be worked into God and mingled with God. When this second aspect is completed, we will be mature in His life. At that time we will express His image and be conformed to His image. When we express His image, spontaneously we also will express His glory. Image and glory are actually one.

GLORY BEING THE SPIRIT SPREADING OUT
FROM WITHIN MAN

The result of being transformed into the Lord's image is that the Lord is expressed from within us. This is the work of the Spirit. At the time of our salvation, the Spirit entered into our spirit. From that time on, the Spirit desires to spread out from our spirit into every part of our being—our mind, emotion, and will. When the Spirit is able to do this, our mind, preferences, and opinions will have the element of the Spirit and will bear traces of the work of the Spirit. Then, whenever someone comes in contact with us, they will sense the flavor of the Spirit in all of our thoughts, preferences, choices, decisions, and opinions. This is because the Spirit has expanded and spread out from within us. The Spirit who has expanded and spread out from within us is our glory.

If we allow the Spirit to do this, others will sense glory with us. They will also feel that we are noble and different. Sometimes we may come in contact with a particular saint whom we know is saved but whose speaking, conduct, thoughts, and sentiments cause us to feel that he is a person who is base and dishonorable. Why is this? It is because he has not allowed the Spirit to spread out from within him to all the parts of his being. On the other hand, sometimes we may contact a saint who does not have a high status in the world but who gives us the sense that he is noble, honorable, weighty, and bright. Although we may be more educated, have more learning, be of a higher status in the world, and be more capable and wealthy than he, we have the sense that we are lower than he is. This sense proves that this person has the glory of God with him.

This glory is the Spirit of God being expressed from within him. Therefore, when people contact him, it is like they are contacting the Lord. When people are with him, they feel that they have the presence of the Lord. This is because this person has the Lord's image. His speaking, opinions, feelings, and moods all have the image of the Lord, because the Lord is being expressed from within him. The glory and image that we sense are the expression of the Spirit, and the Spirit is the Lord Himself (2 Cor. 3:17). Thus, the Lord as the Spirit is manifested from within him. This is a mature person.

GOLD SIGNIFYING
THE LIFE AND NATURE OF GOD

We all know that God works in us in three Persons. He is God, Christ, and the Holy Spirit. These three Persons—the Father, the Son, and the Spirit—are actually one God, the Triune God. The Triune God's purpose is to work Himself into us and also to work Himself out from within us. The apostle Paul said that in God's building, He uses gold, silver, and precious stones as the materials (1 Cor. 3:12). Gold refers to the life and nature of God. At the time we were saved, God entered into us, and we received God's life and nature. God's life and nature are typified by gold. In other words, when we were saved, God added His life and nature into our being as gold.

SILVER SIGNIFYING CHRIST'S REDEMPTION

There is no doubt that every person who has been saved has received God with His life and nature. This is to say, once a person is saved, he experiences the first step of God's work—the element of the Triune God is worked into him and he receives the golden element of God. The second step is the work of silver. This refers to the work of Christ. In the Bible silver refers to redemption, and Christ's redemptive work is the work of the cross. There is a twofold meaning to the cross. On the one hand, it rids us of what we should not have, and on the other hand, it recovers what we originally received that became degraded. These are the two aspects of Christ's redemptive work on the cross.

THE TWO ASPECTS OF CHRIST'S
REDEMPTIVE WORK ON THE CROSS

When God first created us, He gave us everything that we would need. He created for us a mind with the ability to think, an emotion with the ability to love, and a will with the ability to make decisions. We need all of these things, so all of them were created for us by God. However, man fell and all of these items fell into an improper position. Moreover, because man continued to fall, man was mixed up with much uncleanness, sin, and corruption. The redemption of the cross of the Lord Jesus saves us from all the things that we do not need and also recovers the things that we do need, including a normal mind, emotion, and will.

In short, we were created by God with everything that we would need. However, we fell and because of this fall, sin and the world were added into us. The Lord Jesus' redemption on the cross takes away the sins and the world from within us and is recovering us so that we can be used by God. This is the principle of Christ's redemption on the cross. This is the work of silver, of God the Son.

At the time we were saved, God entered into us as the Spirit; thus, we received the golden element of God. Then based upon Christ's redemptive work, every day the cross takes away the sins and the world from within in us and recovers us. When we allow the cross to take away the sins and the world and to recover us back to God in this way, we receive the work of silver and the silver element of Christ. All those who have been fully saved have this silver element. Bit by bit we are allowing the cross to take away the sins and the world from within us and at the same time to recover us back to God.

Some saints, however, do not have this experience of the cross. They have only the golden element; they do not have the silver element. For example, a person who is truly saved and regenerated has the life of God within him. Thus, he has the golden element of God. However, this person is fallen, and he has a weakness. His weakness is that he loses his temper easily. Some have fallen into playing mah-jongg, others have fallen into going to the movies, but this person has fallen into losing his temper. He loses his temper easily. If his wife, children, relatives, colleagues, or even the brothers and sisters displease him in the slightest bit, he loses his temper. He does not care whether this is pleasing to God or what God's will is—his entire person falls into his temper. Such a person is genuinely saved—he has God's golden element—but he does not have Christ's silver element. He has God's life, but he has not experienced the redeeming and dealing work of the cross. He has the golden element but not the silver element.

Although he has allowed the blood of the cross to save him from God's condemnation, he has not allowed the redemptive power of the cross to recover him from his temper. Likewise, some people have not allowed the cross to save them from movie theaters or from their addictions. It would not be fair to say that they have not been saved. However, although they have been saved, they remain in their temper or their addictions. This shows that they have gold in them but not silver. They have the life element of God in them but very little of the work of the cross.

There are some, however, who although they used to have quick tempers, addictions, and different kinds of weaknesses, they have all allowed the cross of Christ to deliver them from all these things. The cross of Christ has saved them from their temper, addictions, and various kinds of wickedness and brought them back to God. The cross has taken away the temper, addictions, and sins that they should not have. At the same time, the cross has also recovered the things that they should have and brought them back to God. Such ones have both gold and silver. Thus, when we come into contact with such persons, we can testify that they have both gold and silver.

PRECIOUS STONES SIGNIFYING
THE CONSTITUTING WORK OF THE HOLY SPIRIT

Is a person mature if he has both the golden nature of God and the silver element of Christ? Is he mature if he has both gold and silver? No, he is not. He still needs precious stones. What kind of work do precious stones represent? Precious stones represent the constituting work of the Holy Spirit within us. A saint who has the golden element of God and the silver redemptive work of Christ does not necessarily resemble the Lord, having the Lord's flavor or the Lord's image. This is because he lacks the constituting work of the Holy Spirit.

First, a believer needs to have the golden element, then he needs the silver element, and third, he needs the precious stones. Gold indicates that he is saved and has the life of God within him. However, at this stage he still may remain in his lust, wickedness, addictions, and temper, because he has not yet received the work of the cross—the silver element. As he is gradually delivered from his lust, wickedness, addictions, and temper, the silver work of the cross will become apparent. Then he will have gold and silver and will no longer have his addictions and wickedness. However, at this stage he may still have his own thoughts and others may not be able to sense any flavor of the Lord in his speaking. Moreover, his opinions may not come from the Lord. Such a person has received the life of God and the dealing work of the cross, but his preferences, emotions, opinions, views, and thoughts do not cause others to sense the Lord's presence. Although his opinions are not wicked, and he does not aspire after the world, others cannot sense the Lord's presence in his expression. This is because he has not received the constituting work of the Holy Spirit.

PRECIOUS STONES NOT BEING CREATED
BUT CONSTITUTED

Precious stones are not originally created by God. People who study chemistry know that precious stones come from materials buried deep in the ground that have undergone burning and high pressure. Similarly, we are not precious stones originally. Our thoughts are not precious stone, our emotions are not precious stone, and our opinions are all the more not precious stone. No matter how good or how lofty they are, their nature is not precious stone. Our mind, emotion, and will are transformed into precious stone by being constituted and burnt by the Holy Spirit and also being pressed by the outward situations.

For example, suppose that you have a very good mind, a very clean emotion, and also a very proper will. Even if this is the case, these things are not precious stones. They are what you originally have in your natural being. They do not have the element of the Lord in them because they lack the work of the Holy Spirit. You have to let the Holy Spirit enter your mind, emotion, and will and allow Him to burn you like fire. You also have to allow the outward situations to coordinate together to deal with you. Through the burning, dealing, pressing, and constituting of the Holy Spirit inside and all the situations outside, your thoughts, emotions, and will receive the element of the Lord and even the Lord Himself. Eventually, this will cause your mind, emotion, and will to become precious stones.

At this point, when a person comes into contact with you, he will feel that you not only have the life of God and the work of the cross but also the Lord Himself in your mind, preferences, and opinions. As soon as a person comes into contact with you, he will feel as if he is coming into contact with the Lord. Spiritually, you will have the shining of the precious stones. Inwardly, you will have gold and silver, and outwardly, you will have the appearance of precious stones. This means that God, Christ, and the Holy Spirit within you will also have worked out of you. This matches the expression of the New Jerusalem in Revelation 21. The brightness of the New Jerusalem is jasper, and jasper is a precious stone. Moreover, the wall of the New Jerusalem is also jasper, and the foundations of the wall are precious stones. In other words, the New Jerusalem is a city of jasper, and jasper is God's expression.

Revelation 4:3 says that He who was sitting on the throne was like a jasper stone and a sardius. This shows that the appearance of the New Jerusalem is the same as that of

God—both are jasper and precious stones. Precious stones are produced by the constituting work of the Holy Spirit. Therefore, the appearance of precious stones is also an issue of the constituting work of the Holy Spirit. This appearance is the expression of the Holy Spirit. This entirely echoes 2 Corinthians 3 which says that the expression of the Holy Spirit from within us is the shining and image, and this shining and image are the Lord Himself. Thus, we can see from Revelation that the appearance of the New Jerusalem is jasper and precious stones and that the appearance of jasper and precious stones is also the appearance of the Lord who is sitting on the throne.

THE WORK OF GOLD, SILVER, AND PRECIOUS STONES

How can we become like the Lord? How can we have the image of God? The first step is to let God's life, which is the Spirit, enter into us. In this way we will have gold in us. Then we need to let the cross work in us, separate us from sins, the world, lust, and our preferences. Is this separation by the cross sufficient? It is not. The Holy Spirit still needs to constitute us and burn within our mind, emotion, will, and entire inner being. Together with the pressing work of the outward environment, the work of the Holy Spirit will work the Lord's image as a precious stone into us. This transforms us into precious stones. When that time comes, God will have completed His work in us, and we will be mature.

There are three steps to the work of the Triune God—the Father, Son, and Spirit. We were originally created by God to contain God. However, we fell into sins and the world. So one day God came to redeem us and cleanse us with the blood of His Son. Moreover, He put His life and nature, His golden element, into us. Thus, we were regenerated and saved. From then on Christ's cross has been carrying out its separating work in us so that we are separated time and time again from sins, the world, temper, and lust and are placed on God's side. Then the Holy Spirit burns within us and carries out a constituting work within us. Because we are rebellious and resistant, the Holy Spirit also uses the outward environment in coordination with His work within us to burn us, press us, and constitute us to the extent that our mind, emotion, and will all have the shining image of God and become like precious stones, that is, resemble the Lord. This image is the image of the glory of the Lord. This is what it means to be transformed into the image of the Lord, even as from the Lord Spirit.

By this time we will not only have gold and silver but also precious stones. We will be bright and honorable. When people come into contact with us, they will sense the Lord's presence. We will have the image of the Lord, and our speaking and expression will have the flavor of the Lord. Our thoughts, emotions, opinions, views, and choices will also have the Lord's flavor. Even those who do not like us will respect us from deep within because we will have weight before the Lord and will have been constituted with the Holy Spirit. We will have the brightness of precious stones, which is the image of the Lord.

HOW THE HOLY SPIRIT CONSTITUTES WITHIN US

How does the Holy Spirit constitute and burn within us? The Lord loves and cares for each one of us. We have all been saved and have the life of the Lord. We are also willing to let Christ's cross work within us. Thus, we have gold and also silver. But this is not enough. We all need to have the experience of the precious stones. We are now undergoing the process of becoming precious stones. Although we have not experienced sufficient burning, sufficient pressing, and sufficient constituting, we are in this process. The Holy Spirit is operating and constituting within all of us.

For example, suppose we dislike someone, and the mere sight of this person annoys us. At this point, the Holy Spirit will begin to work within us. If we dislike someone, the Holy Spirit will give us a sense within and cause us to feel that it is not right for us to dislike this person and that our dislike does not come from the Lord. The Holy Spirit will bother us, stir within us, and at the same time will constitute us with Himself so that we will be knit together with Him. The Holy Spirit will bother us today, stir within us tomorrow, operate within us the day after, and burn within us a few days later.

Then bit by bit, after a few months we will no longer dislike that person as much as we did before. However, we still may not like him—some feeling may still remain within us. Therefore, the Holy Spirit will raise up the environment. He will hit us on the left, press us on the right, and cause us to suffer from some illness or to encounter some other difficulty. The Holy Spirit will deal with us outwardly in this way. Then one day, without knowing why, our dislike for this person will disappear, and when we see him, we will even think that he is nice and gentle. Moreover, when we see him again at another time, we will even be able to have good fellowship with him. This is the constituting work of the Holy Spirit within us.

Having been burnt, constituted, and pressed by the Holy Spirit, our emotions and preferences, as well as our mind, thoughts, will, and opinions, will have the flavor of the Lord. Very often, our mind and thoughts do not have the Holy Spirit. They are simply our own thoughts, thoughts that are according to the ways of the world. Therefore, the Holy Spirit will touch us—bothering, turning, and stirring within us—and ask us, "Is this the Lord's way? Is this the Lord's truth? Is this the Lord's method?" If we do not listen to these questions and this speaking inside of us, an outward environment will come to hit us, press us, and deal with us. Eventually, all we will be able to do will be to bow down before the Lord. Our mind will have been smitten, our emotion broken, and our will defeated. Now we will have the Lord's image, and everything that comes from our mind, emotion, and will shall be like precious stones—being glorious and bearing the Lord's presence. This will be the expression of the Holy Spirit and the image of the Lord.

Revelation tells us that the New Jerusalem is a golden mountain. The street of the city is pure gold, and the wall of the city is jasper. This depicts the work of the Holy Spirit within us. At the time of our salvation, we receive the gold inside of us but not the wall outside of us or the image of the Lord. Thus, the Holy Spirit will work in us further until bit by bit our mind, emotion, and will receive the Lord's image. When we receive the Lord's image, we will have the wall, precious stones, and glory. All these things are the expression of the Lord and are God Himself. The precious stones are the image of God, the manifestation of God. This is what it means to be mature.

ABOUT THE AUTHOR

Witness Lee was born in 1905 in northern China and raised in a Christian family. At age 19 he was fully captured for Christ and immediately consecrated himself to preach the gospel for the rest of his life. Early in his service, he met Watchman Nee, a renowned preacher, teacher, and writer. Witness Lee labored together with Watchman Nee under his direction. In 1934 Watchman Nee entrusted Witness Lee with the responsibility for his publication operation, called the Shanghai Gospel Bookroom.

Prior to the Communist takeover in 1949, Witness Lee was sent by Watchman Nee and his other co-workers to Taiwan to insure that the things delivered to them by the Lord would not be lost. Watchman Nee instructed Witness Lee to continue the former's publishing operation abroad as the Taiwan Gospel Bookroom, which has been publicly recognized as the publisher of Watchman Nee's works outside China. Witness Lee's work in Taiwan manifested the Lord's abundant blessing. From a mere 350 believers, newly fled from the mainland, the churches in Taiwan grew to 20,000 in five years.

In 1962 Witness Lee felt led of the Lord to come to the United States, settling in California. During his 35 years of service in the U.S., he ministered in weekly meetings and weekend conferences, delivering several thousand spoken messages. Much of his speaking has since been published as over 400 titles. Many of these have been translated into over fourteen languages. He gave his last public conference in February 1997 at the age of 91.

He leaves behind a prolific presentation of the truth in the Bible. His major work, *Life-study of the Bible,* comprises over 25,000 pages of commentary on every book of the Bible from the perspective of the believers' enjoyment and experience of God's divine life in Christ through the Holy Spirit. Witness Lee was the chief editor of a new translation of the New Testament into Chinese called the Recovery Version and directed the translation of the same into English. The Recovery Version also appears in a number of other languages. He provided an extensive body of footnotes, outlines, and spiritual cross references. A radio broadcast of his messages can be heard on Christian radio stations in the United States. In 1965 Witness Lee founded Living Stream Ministry, a non-profit corporation, located in Anaheim, California, which officially presents his and Watchman Nee's ministry.

Witness Lee's ministry emphasizes the experience of Christ as life and the practical oneness of the believers as the Body of Christ. Stressing the importance of attending to both these matters, he led the churches under his care to grow in Christian life and function. He was unbending in his conviction that God's goal is not narrow sectarianism but the Body of Christ. In time, believers began to meet simply as the church in their localities in response to this conviction. In recent years a number of new churches have been raised up in Russia and in many eastern European countries.

OTHER BOOKS PUBLISHED BY
Living Stream Ministry

Titles by Witness Lee:

Abraham—Called by God	0-7363-0359-6
The Experience of Life	0-87083-417-7
The Knowledge of Life	0-87083-419-3
The Tree of Life	0-87083-300-6
The Economy of God	0-87083-415-0
The Divine Economy	0-87083-268-9
God's New Testament Economy	0-87083-199-2
The World Situation and God's Move	0-87083-092-9
Christ vs. Religion	0-87083-010-4
The All-inclusive Christ	0-87083-020-1
Gospel Outlines	0-87083-039-2
Character	0-87083-322-7
The Secret of Experiencing Christ	0-87083-227-1
The Life and Way for the Practice of the Church Life	0-87083-785-0
The Basic Revelation in the Holy Scriptures	0-87083-105-4
The Crucial Revelation of Life in the Scriptures	0-87083-372-3
The Spirit with Our Spirit	0-87083-798-2
Christ as the Reality	0-87083-047-3
The Central Line of the Divine Revelation	0-87083-960-8
The Full Knowledge of the Word of God	0-87083-289-1
Watchman Nee—A Seer of the Divine Revelation...	0-87083-625-0

Titles by Watchman Nee:

How to Study the Bible	0-7363-0407-X
God's Overcomers	0-7363-0433-9
The New Covenant	0-7363-0088-0
The Spiritual Man 3 volumes	0-7363-0269-7
Authority and Submission	0-7363-0185-2
The Overcoming Life	1-57593-817-0
The Glorious Church	0-87083-745-1
The Prayer Ministry of the Church	0-87083-860-1
The Breaking of the Outer Man and the Release...	1-57593-955-X
The Mystery of Christ	1-57593-954-1
The God of Abraham, Isaac, and Jacob	0-87083-932-2
The Song of Songs	0-87083-872-5
The Gospel of God 2 volumes	1-57593-953-3
The Normal Christian Church Life	0-87083-027-9
The Character of the Lord's Worker	1-57593-322-5
The Normal Christian Faith	0-87083-748-6
Watchman Nee's Testimony	0-87083-051-1

Available at
Christian bookstores, or contact Living Stream Ministry
2431 W. La Palma Ave. • Anaheim, CA 92801
1-800-549-5164 • www.livingstream.com